Bows of the World

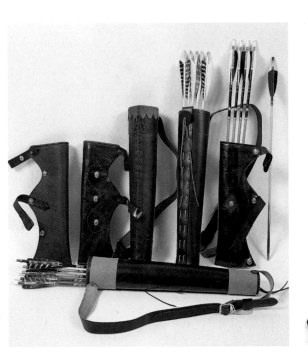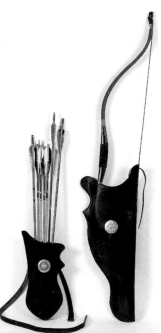

Bows of the World

David Gray

The Lyons Press

Guilford, Connecticut

An Imprint of the Globe Pequot Press

Contents

Acknowledgments

I am indebted to many people for nurturing my love and knowledge of archery. Some of the mentors and friends who have taught me over a thirty-year period will be mentioned by name, but I'm sure I am neglecting many others. Here are two important people I want to thank: my father for giving me the run of the farm and the freedom during my boyhood to cut hickory saplings for bows and apple shoots for arrows; and my wife Phyllis for giving me my first adult bow as well as continual encouragement.

Also, much is owed to my close association with fellow North Americans Jaap and Kay Koppedayer, Lukas Novotny, Tony Horvath, Mark Gabel, Larry Snell, Manuel Lizzaralde, and Todd Delle. I have tested and promoted many more products from bowyers, quiver makers, and arrow makers, and my appreciation of the diversity of archery is the direct result.

In Hungary, Kassai Lajos opened up the entire world of horseback archery for me, and that includes his wonderful valley. Jan Bisok from the foothills of the Tatras gave me an invaluable perspective on Polish archery, with many thanks to Malgosia Fialkowska who facilitated my Polish activities. Much appreciation also goes to friends in England: Neil Beeby, Chris Boyton, Ted Bradford, Victor Cole, Doug Elmy, Hilary Greenland, and Richard Head. While Flemming Alrune in Denmark helped greatly in the Scandinavian portion of my research, and France's Thomas Kuhn offered many leads on printed sources.

On the other side of the globe, however, Lawrence Allen from Australia patiently initiated me into the lore of historical Japanese arrows, while Thomas Selby made so much more available the historical riches of Chinese archery. Likewise, Thomas Duverney brought Korean bows and the tradition of archery out in the open for all.

Surely all archers are indebted to Jim Hamm and associates for producing *The Traditional Bowyer's Bible*. My own sampling of world bows would not have been possible without all the other archery authors cited herein. I have drawn heavily from a number of journals, including the oldest continuous publication *Journal of the Society of Archer Antiquaries*. The wealth of information provided by the editors and authors of this, as well as other, traditional archery magazines was essential.

The interlibrary loan service through Westminster College (PA) made some hard-to-obtain sources easily available. The Griffith Institute in England was also most cooperative in granting permission to reproduce plates.

And finally, thank you, Phyllis, for proofing and improving my writing. The final errors are, of course, all mine.

Kassai Lajos with some of his horses in front of his Yurt in Kaposmero, Hungary.

Introduction

Traditional archery is an art, a philosophy, and even a way of life. The Japanese word for archery (Kyudo) literally means "the way of the bow." The art of archery, however, is not limited to the hunt. Many use it for recreational purposes, others as a means of relaxation. But for nearly all it is an avenue of self-development. Meaning so much to so many, bows throughout history, and throughout the world, can help us understand more about ourselves and our neighbors.

In that endeavor, this book is limited to an exploration of traditional archery. Traditional archery, however, does not include bows with pulleys and multiple cables that magnify the arrow's thrust, or with balances that dampen torque or other errors of form. Nor should the term "traditional" include bows with sights, or those that are shot with mechanical releases, other than gloves, tabs, or thumb rings. In short, all compound bows and all non-compound Olympic-style target bows (which use mechanical aids) are beyond the scope of this book.

At the same time, I include myself among those sports enthusiasts who respect the performance of those types of bows in the hands of disciplined and accomplished archers. While personal interest is largely limited to traditional archery, I sincerely hope tolerance and even appreciation for all forms of archery will grow everywhere.

So, when I use the word "traditional," it should include the category of bow commonly referred to as "primitive." The latter tends to refer to bows made of one piece of wood that has had a minimal amount of power machining. The connotation of primitive, then should be "earliest, prime, or first," rather than the more frequent connotation of "less well developed," since I believe the engineering of the primitive bow was relatively sophisticated, especially given the raw materials available.

A Mirror of Early Human Achievement

The creativity, adaptability, and downright intelligence of our ancient forefathers are indelibly stamped upon their tools and weapons—certainly upon the artifacts of their archery. Variations of the highly effective flatbow are believed to have been in use at least 10,000 years ago, possibly even earlier. One longbow that had a nearly round cross section (and often a somewhat flattened back) appears in the hands of very early archers around the world—the Nubians in Africa, the Anglo-Saxons, the ancient Egyptians, the Pueblo and Pima Native North Americans, and many Native South Americans. Beyond the self-bows crafted from a single piece of wood, there are several occurrences of rich and elaborate designs that use horn, sinew, multiple kinds of wood, and many kinds of finishes and decorations. Throughout the world these archery achievements attest to the sophistication of the human mind and spirit. Even in the early prehistoric eras, well-designed bows and arrows were used effectively in tribal warfare and in the critical pursuit of food. Artifacts left behind

Two Wampanoag bows (Sudbury) by Paul Rodgers, an Eva Reed split oak quiver, and a Delaware arrow by Rob Young.

in arid caves, bogs, and tar pits, indicate that our forbears were inventive and capable creatures.

Despite the bow's more utilitarian qualities, its aesthetic value is just as important to ancient and modern archery. The lines and configuration of most bows, whether unstrung, braced, or at full draw, qualify them as a highly developed form of sculpture. This holds true whether or not additional adornment has been added. How many three-dimensional art pieces, after all, require a dynamic shape that can efficiently store energy and release it in a strictly prescribed manner? View the bow in this light and you may think of the bow as the queen of the arts. The sophisticated color patterns the Native Americans added, or the intricate Inuit cabling, even the magnificent Persian gilded lettering and decor only add to the celebration these works of art demand. Traditional archery, whether ancient or modern, has enormous potential to deepen our respect for the human race across time and around the world.

Personal Development

Archery is an ancient art of self-development that embraces discipline, patience, fitness, endurance, beauty, and character. It is one avenue of developing the self in body, mind, and spirit. These goals are explicit in the Japanese martial art of Kyudo, and they are implicit for all archers. The challenge of training oneself to master a primitive and traditional weapon is balanced by its enjoyment and lifelong satisfaction. Respect for one's self and for others seems to be a by-product of the respect traditional bowyers and archers have learned for a skill that cannot be rushed. The skill behind shooting a traditional bow comes slowly and patiently, and demands unflagging pursuit. Confidence, another by-product of this skill, is evident when the bull's eye is struck with a tight group of arrows. At the same time, however, this respect and confidence tends to be low on arrogance and high on harmony, a unity with all of life.

A Universal Language

While archery training is done in solitude, it's another of the many "universal languages" that bring people together. Olympic archery has been doing this for a long time, and national boundaries are increasingly being crossed in the more traditional archery circles. Of the half-dozen or so widely known journals devoted to traditional archery in Europe and the United States, all include a broad human-interest dimension, and they are increasingly international.

A story about a particular bow will most likely be told against the background of the history, conditions, and characteristics of its bowyer, its archer, and the people of its region. We can only know a fraction of a bow's story if we do not know the story of its people. Contributors to these journals strive for authenticity, and respect the lives in the larger context of their stories. Admittedly, however, the emphasis on acquiring a trophy sometimes overshadows the story's more important aspects. Generally, the journals recite the histories of very different cultures, outlining their different raw materials, and the diverse climates they lived in when selecting the materials and creating the designs that would result in effective weapons.

Likewise, hunting accounts in these journals take the reader all over the world. Exotic hunting trips, however, are often as not told of by ordinary people—rather than just by celebrities, which was more common in the past. As such, the hunting tales told by traditional archers usually emphasize the challenge, stimulation, and discipline of the hunt rather than just trophy gathering. In these stories, sound hunting ethics and sensitivity for indigenous people and their land are prominent.

Richard Head English longbow handle detail, an irresistible invitation to traditional archery.

Yet competitive target shooting can also transport the reader to exotic locales. In fact, the leading archery magazine based in England, *The Glade*, carries the global subtitle, "The International Archery Magazine." Although this journal usually covers compound and Olympic-like target events, traditional practices are also covered. All in all the coverage is far more international than sports such as American football or baseball.

The largest traditional archery shoots in the U.S. typically attract participants from across the globe. International archery equipment is also much more readily available today via catalogs, Web sites, and international dealers. The revival of mounted archery, for instance, clearly has an international thrust. The first demonstration of the standardized European version of mounted archery occurred in the summer of 1998 at the Michigan Longbow Invitational. Kassai Lajos, the founder of modern European mounted archery, thrilled the crowd and opened what will likely be an exciting new element in the growth of traditional archery. Two young Lakota Sioux who trained in mounted archery with Kassai at the First International Horse Archery Festival here in the States travelled to Hungary for a full week of intensive training—a dramatic and positive instance of mixed cultures and widened horizons among traditional archers.

The rediscovery of primitive archery not only has the potential to bring people together, but its inherent dynamic can force us to examine our place in the larger community of nature. The discipline of ecology tells us that we are not discontinuous with the rest of nature, that we are interdependent with it. The primitive bowyer and archer depend upon select trees for wood, stone for points, animals for horn, glue, sinew, skin, and feathers, even the soil, air, and water—in short the community of life and land.

Bows of the World

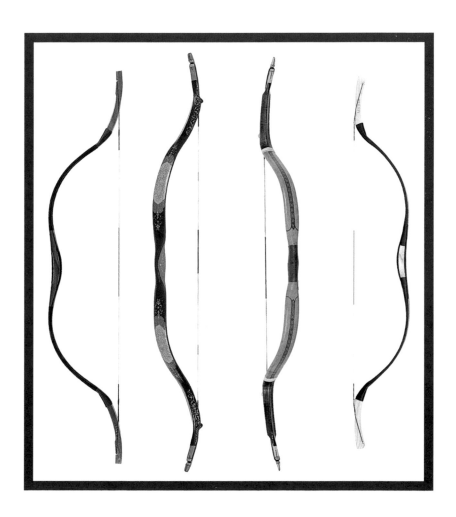

Holmegaard handle detail: significant early development of a non-working handle to reduce hand shock.

1 · Prehistoric Bows

It's no secret that relatively perishable materials such as wood, papyrus, and fabric from prehistoric time may survive under certain conditions. Abnormally dry layers of earth in arid caves have preserved papyrus and fabric. Peat bogs, especially in northern Europe, have yielded many wood artifacts, some of which are clearly the remains of ancient bows. These artifacts are usually pieces of broken bows, but complete or almost complete bows are not uncommon. Still, whether or not these artifacts were indeed bows is certain in some cases and arguable in others. This is an exciting place to begin an earnest observation of early human potential and achievement.

The thrill of holding a faithful replica of an elm bow, and experiencing the lives of our ancestors 9,000 years ago, has been felt by only a few archers. To draw that bow (the Holmegaard bow, for instance) and let the arrow fly with such force and accuracy brings a rare kind of rush. The ancient archer's heart and soul have long been gone, but I feel at one with him. I feel I know something about that person's intelligence and spirit. This is not a crude weapon. It is of sound design and delivers the typical modern target arrow at 150 feet per second (at a draw of 50 pounds at 27 inches).

Although we insist, however inaccurately, on drawing a sharp distinction between scientific and pre-scientific humans, this ancient archer—isolated from modern physics, calculus, and modern technology by millennia—still possessed a rudimentary measurement system and an elementary kind of trial-and-error approach to applied physical science that served him well. Aristotle is often given credit for the first systematic observation and classification of flora, but judging from their bows, ancient northern Europeans knew enough to differentiate between the many kinds of plants and trees. Furthermore, they demonstrate a significant grasp of technology in using these natural materials to construct tools. Not unrelated here is the recent definitive evidence of the sophisticated plant classification used by the the supposedly underdeveloped indigenous Ka'apor people in Brazil and Venezuela.

Four bows are featured in this chapter—Stellmoor, Holmegaard, Mere Heath, and Ashcott. Substantial pieces of each of these bows have been identified with certainty. The Stellmoor bow, however, is an exception, since only short limb pieces have been found.

Stellmoor

In a 1943 report, Alfred Rust described artifacts taken from bogs in northern Germany; they included notched arrow shafts, arrow points, and two pieces of wood that look like limb tips of a stone-age bow. If these pieces are bow fragments, they are probably about 11,000 years old. One piece is about ten inches (24.8cm) long and the other about seven inches (18cm) at about $3/4$ inch (2 to 2.5cm) wide. Flint tips, of course, could have meant a small spear or atlatl. But the limbs taper very gradually toward the ends to a $3/4$ inch dimension, with more abrupt tapering at the last couple of inches. Wounds in bird skeletons further convinced Rust that the points must have been archery-based, and that the wood fragments were portions of bows.

Two older authorities on stone-age archery confirmed they were bow fragments (Clark, 1963, and Rausing, 1997), and Comstock (1993) agrees. Insulander (1999) furthered the diagnosis, stipulating that they were made from pine, which would be durable if it was the compression-wood portion (not heartwood) taken from a leaning tree. Alrune's (1996) expertise led him to say that he would ..."not reject the two pieces as possible remains of bows, but leave it open to further debate and study."

The Holmegaard

This is the type of ancient bow referred to in this chapter's introduction. Two artifacts of the Holmegaard were found in a bog in 1943 during the process of cutting peat. The bog site is about 50 miles southwest of Copenhagen, which is on the Danish Island called Zealand. One of the bows found there is complete, and apparently the very oldest complete bow found in the world to this date. It is about 5½ feet or 154 cm. The other artifact is only half of a bow, but in its complete form it would have been considerably longer, estimated to have been between 66 and 70 inches (170 to 180 cm). About 9,000 years old, the artifacts are preserved in the National Museum in Copenhagen.

Flemming Alrune (1996) has become a leading voice on the Holmegaard. He lives in Haslev, not far from the Holmegaard bog, and cuts his elm saplings close to where the artifacts were retrieved. From the photos, one notices the Holmegaard's unique architecture. Looking at the bow from the back or the belly, the limbs narrow abruptly around the midpoint (along a distance of about 2½ inches). Looking from the edge, the handle gradually tapers, as usual to the limb midpoint, where it actually thickens just perceptibly, and then flows almost parallel to the tips.

What was probably the belly of the bow is flat, and the back is convex, following the outer growth rings of the sapling in the traditional manner. Differentiating the back from the belly, however, has been controversial. Volume 2 of the *Bowyer's Bible* (1993, page 91) shows that the bow was actually reversed—the back being flat. Alrune and Callahan, however, are convinced that the bow was not reversed.

Belly view of Holmegaard by Flemming Alrune. Notice the unusual abrupt constriction at the mid-limb area.

This rather unusual design has appeared in other Danish finds such as Tybring Vig and Vidbaek, and has endured for about 3,000 years (Callahan, 1996). Either the design was sound, or the bowyers were unimaginative. Some of the modern reconstructions tend to start stacking (the fairly sudden increase in resistance towards the later part of the draw) at about 26 inches, but they are accurate and fast for an ancient self-bow, and were probably used by archers considerably shorter than today's, with considerably shorter draws. Athough Alrune is a thorough, and cautious worker, his praise for reconstructions is liberal. He has made many reconstructions himself and says that, in his opinion "their design, durability, and performance has not been excelled to the present" (1996). Lengthening the reconstructions to 72 inches or so, however, fits a taller modern archer who wants to pull a traditional 27- or 28-inch draw, and would undoubtedly eliminate stiffness or stacking.

My own reconstruction of the Holmegaard (pictured, made by Alrune), is 69 inches (175cm) and was chosen for my tall, long-armed stature. Some mild hand shock occurs at my 27-inch draw, but it is very accurate, has a crisp cast, and only developed about an inch of string follow after considerable test shooting. Made from an elm sapling seasoned for two years, it's strung with Irish flax treated with beeswax, and there are no nock grooves. Instead, the string rests on sinew bulbs. This reconstruction is patterned after the half-bow found in the Holmegaard bog, and it's not difficult to appreciate the elegance and performance of this weapon.

The design and sculpt of this type of bow in no way reflects a dull, simple-minded craftsman. Mixed with what must have been great superstition these ancient people had a keen imagination, a well developed intelligence, and a clever method of rudimentary experiment. There is no room for condescension in light of their achievements. Here "primitive" cannot mean "crude" or "rudely simple," but "first" or "earliest," that from

Holmegaard showing thickening of limbs in the last 12 inches leading to the tips (side view).

which later forms are "derived." Their mechanical expertise was among the best of that early technology, and their artistic sense was just as admirable. The Holmegaard, after all, is a beautiful, working piece of dynamic sculpture.

I will not over-romanticize the 9,000-year-old people of the Holmegaard bog, but they demand my respect for their accomplishments in archery.

The following bow remnants come to us from between 4,000 and 5,000 years ago.

The Meare Heath

In 1961, an English peat company discovered two very significant bows, or the pieces thereof, in the southwest corner of England. They were pulled from two different bogs a few miles apart—one in the Meare Heath, the other in the Ashcott Heath. Heaths are open areas, often covered with heather and other shrubs, so these locations were centered in Glastonbury in the Somerset County lowlands, or "Levels," some 20 miles south of Bristol. Thanks to the sensitivity of the workers extracting the peat, the remains were safely and quickly transported to skilled archeological experts at Cambridge University, where they still reside in the University's Museum of Archeology and Ethnography. In both cases, only one-half of a bow was recovered, each broken at what appears to be mid-handle.

The Meare artifact dates to 2690 B.C., with a 120-year error term plus or minus by radiocarbon testing. This is confirmed by strata dating and plant residue on the staves. So again, we have a window into the life of the archers, bowyers, and ancients of nearly 5,000 years ago. About half of the handle is extant; the full limb is quite well preserved, yet the nock is only partial.

This is a huge bow, probably about 71 inches (190cm) or more. The limb configurations are very wide, $2^{19}/_{32}$ inches (6.85cm) at the widest and a very thin $^{19}/_{32}$ inches (1.75cm). The limbs also taper into a very definite handle section about an inch wide. In the other direction, the limbs taper extremely gradually ending at a width of about $1^{1}/_{2}$ inches at the nock. In other words, at first glace the limb edges seem to remain nearly parallel to the very tips. In cross section, the back is convex and the belly is nearly flat. The side view shows that the limbs taper gradually from the handle to the tip, following the string a little, and the handle is just noticeably backset. This is interesting because of the difficulty in building it. The large amount of mass in the ends of the limbs and the excessive length for a flatbow must have reduced its efficiency.

The bow's appearance is also unique because of the limb wrappings. Impressions on the limbs show that both leather strips and some type of "thread" were used. Eight or nine transverse wraps of ox-skin encircle the limbs about equidistant from each other, and in between these bands a thread is cross wrapped as well. Most evaluations deny that the binding enhanced durability or performance, so the decor may point to ceremonial, sacrificial, or burial use. As Hilary Greenland says, however, the bow as a whole is an enigma, and it may be whatever one wants it to be.

Ashcott Heath

In contrast to the Meare Heath, the Ashcott is about a foot shorter (30cm). Instead of being wide in limb, however, it is only about 1 inch at mid-limb, tapering to about $\frac{5}{8}$ inch at the nock. The handle area may have been slightly more than 1 inch, and the limbs cross section is a "D." The Ashcott dating (2665 B.C.) is very close to the Meare bow, and both were made from the interior portion of a major yew tree.

Just as Flemming Alrune has become identified with the Holmegaard find so close to his residence, so Hilary Greenland seems to be identified with the Meare and Ashcott findings just south of her home base in Bristol. Greenland has re-created working bows from both of these models and documented their performance to the enrichment of Toxophilites everywhere. Although she actually seems to favor the Holmegaard a little more, she has demonstrated the viability as well as the limitations of both bows. Others, of course, have replicated many of these pre-historic bows. In the States, the work of Paul Comstock and Tim Baker represents a very significant and lasting contribution to our understanding of archery's ancient roots.

Other Pre-historic European Bows

There may be nearly a hundred Stone Age and older artifacts from Europe. The finds cluster in the lowlands, the bogs of southern England, Denmark, and northern Germany, and around the Swiss lakes. In most cases, the artifacts are bow fragments. E. G. Heath (1972) gives a nice map revealing the locations of the findings across Europe.

Gad Rausing lists 22 finds from the Swiss lake area, all of them of yew wood and all with the "D" cross section. One full bow was 70 inches long, but most of them pointed to a length of about 60 inches. The other sites are most concentrated in the northwest quadrant of the continent—Holland, northern Germany, England, and Scandinavia. Artifacts from this region come in a variety of styles; the "D" cross section is again very much in evidence, but the flat bow is also very common.

The famed medieval English longbow, with the deeply stacked D cross section, developed over a long period of time and geographic scope. The English refinements and modifications were nevertheless significant and will be discussed in the chapter on Europe. The parallel development of the flatbow in pre-historic Europe and much later in North America is apparently not connected in any way.

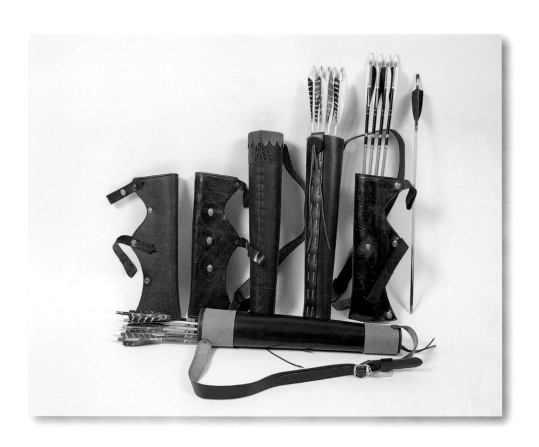

Six artistically crafted quivers by Larry Snell of Indiana. The two on the left are belt quivers of Asian influence.

2 · The Americas

Every imaginable modern North American bow will be on display as one walks through the vendors' area at one of the world's largest traditional archery meets, namely the Eastern Traditional Archery Rendezvous in Coudersport, Pennsylvania. Native North Americans and their bows are more abundant at an event such as the International Horse Archery Festival in Fort Dodge, Iowa. The selections in this chapter begin with the Native North American bows, then North American bows, and ends with selections from South America.

North America

In keeping with the idea that one cannot appreciate the bows of a people without having a sense of the people and their place in the stream of history, we need to "fast rewind" to the likely origins of the Native Americans. Somewhere between 30,000 to 15,000 years ago, a mostly solid ice-covered passageway extended over the Bering Strait from Asia to what, much later, came to bear the name North America. Many anthropologists contend that a number of migrations of northern Asian peoples crossed this land bridge and disseminated across North and South America. American and Russian scientists assert that human skull and teeth remains indicate that the Paleo-Indians derived from northern Asians of the larger Siberian region. Some groups stayed in the icy upper reaches of North America, and others pressed ahead in fits and starts to more southern destinations. Prior experience, adaptability, and climatic and survival pressures probably all played a role in determining who left and who stayed.

The latest American migrations were probably about 15,000 years ago. Five thousand years later these groups had pushed south into New Mexico, even to the lower tip of South America. Estimates for the length of human occupation in these areas are generated from radio-carbon tests of Folsom and Clovis spear points, and campfire ashes, as well as through archeological context and layer dating.

A stone weight was often used when throwing a spear with a lever (or atlatl), a practice which can be dated to about 8,000 years ago in North America (and at least twice that age among the Paleolithic hunters in northern Europe). Beyond that, however, what dates do stone points establish for the emergence of the bow and the arrow in North America? Apparently not until relatively late, during the Middle Woodland period, 1-1000 A.D.

At least two American Indian groups have myths that tell of the great migration across the ice. In the Blackfoot oral tradition, the story is called, "Old Man Leads a Migration." It begins, "The first Indians were on the other side of the ocean, and Old Man decided to lead them to a better place. So he brought them over the ice to the far north." It seems to be widely accepted as a genuine Blackfoot myth, but its interpretation has to be left open and mysterious. What do "ocean" and "ice" really mean? There is a very long and detailed account of the migration associated with the Delaware (Lenape) called the *Walam Olum*, but neither the remaining Lenape nor the ethnographic scholars have any confidence that it is an authentic account. Native Americans' tales of their own origins are greatly varied, but many of them locate the site of their creation or emergence within the land they occupied before the time of Columbus. The source of their origins according to their myths includes a great log, a turtle, or mother earth herself.

Bows of the Woodland Peoples

The Woodland people inhabited the vast originally forested region of the United States—nearly one-third of the land mass from the Atlantic coast and westward. The Woodland bows seem to have had the greatest impact on the revival of traditional archery in America. The English-type longbow, on the other hand, was made most dominant in this revival's first wave in the very early 1900s by legends such as the Thompson brothers, Saxton Pope, and Glenn St. Charles. Yet, the practice of flattening the cross section to create what has often been called the American longbow surely owes much of its inspiration to the traditionally flattened Woodland, and Plains, bows of the Native Americans.

What we know of the Woodland bow comes from the many specimens held in museums, only a tiny portion of which are put on display. We have also amassed much of the lore from private collections, the oral traditions of old timers, early ethnographic writings such as those in the Smithsonian collection, and drawings and paintings remaining from the 1800s. Of course, these are the same sources of documentation for all the other Native North American bows as well.

The Algonkian (Lenape, and Mohegan)

For two seasons, I have hunted whitetail deer with an Algonkian bow made by Rob Young in Idaho, and with total confidence. It is 65 inches long nock to nock unstrung, exactly one inch wide uniformly throughout its whole length, $3/4$ inch thick at the center, $3/8$ inch thick at the end of the working limbs, and slightly recurved starting four inches from the tip. There is no riser or sudden thickening in the handle, thus it is a "D" bow in the sense of bending through the handle when drawn. The wood is black locust; it pulled 50 pounds at 28 inches when made, and the cross section is a rectangle.

This bow has a special place in my heart. It's the kind the Native Americans would have used three hundred years ago in my home state, Pennsylvania. Although "D" bows have a reputation for hand shock, this bow shoots comfortably and has a good caste even with a $2^1/2$-inch string follow. The carved human figure at the tips may represent the "Spirit watching over the hunt." On the back is carved a turtle, and the bow hand is placed just

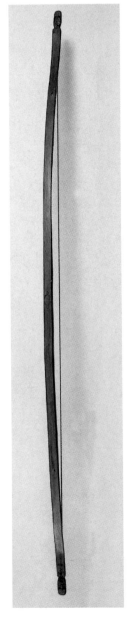

This simple, elegant Algonkian weapon with parallel edged limbs and carving at tips and handle, was made by Rob Young of Idaho.

under it. In many creation myths, the turtle is often a symbol of the "foundation" of the earth. Some extant cemeteries in China, in fact, are shaped like turtles, so the Asian connection appears again.

The dimensions of the Lenape and Mohegan bows are nearly identical to the Algonkian, varying only in tip carvings and types of decorations painted on the back. An Algonkian bow pictured in Allely and Hamm has a simple and beautiful red painting on its back—a geometric serpent figure running the full length of the bow, with dots accenting through the highs and lows of each cycle of the wave or serpent. This adornment strikes me as having a subdued elegance and unspoiled sophistication. While artistic taste is personal and culturally specific, we are once again confronted with evidence that these people were not aesthetically asleep. Handling these bows confronts the ignorance of the Colonists when they described the natives of this country as "...entirely savage and wild, strangers to all decency, yea, uncivil and stupid as garden poles" (Kraft, page 2).

In the following section, we will highlight some of the typical differences between the northern and southern Woodland styles, but the overlap of design in the north and south is probably far greater than the differences. A careful examination by Allely and Hamm reveals the great similarities. We must also remind ourselves that there must have been a great deal of variation within any one tribe, even within the work of a given bowyer.

Cherokee Bows

In 1830, the Indian Removal Bill was passed by the United States Legislature forcing the Cherokees to march on the "trail of tears" to the Oklahoma Territory. In was a death march for about four thousand in the late fall and winter of that year. Gold had been discovered in Georgia, and the white intruders envied the land, desiring to add to their lucrative plantations. By this time, the Cherokee had become peaceful, educated, and productive farmers and crafts persons. All eastern American Indian groups were forcefully moved west of the Mississippi, including the Creeks, the Chickasaws, and the Seminoles, and the northeastern groups were forced to move as well. It was America's holocaust—targeting a specific race, banishing them from their homeland, and causing much suffering and widespread death in the process.

The western Cherokees are unique, however, in that they have maintained much of their original culture, and this is certainly true of their archery. In an unbroken tradition, they make their own style of bow and use it for hunting

This Cherokee bow bends throughout, including the handle section. Made by the eastern Cherokees in North Carolina.

and recreation. Each September in Oklahoma's eastern edge, the Tahlequah region, the bands come together for the traditional cornstalk shoot. A cube of cornstalks, three feet square and one foot thick, forms the face of the target. The archers shoot from 80 yards, and score not only for hitting the face, but also for the degree of penetration. As far as I know, the tribe has, for the very first time, made participation open to any archer by taking the event to the First Annual International Horseback Archery Festival in Fort Dodge, Iowa.

If there is a design weakness in the Algonkian bow, it's that it is too narrow, putting too much compression stress on a rather narrow band of belly wood. The Cherokee bow remedied that with greater width, about 1$\frac{1}{2}$ inches, while being considerably thinner, about $\frac{9}{16}$ inches at the handle, depending on the weight of the bow. With no handle, the Cherokee bow bends throughout that center area. Al Herrin argues this bow's length should be determined by draw length; for example 28 inches times a factor of 2.14 equals 60 inches. The 2.14 factor reflects the old rule of thumb that a self-bow should be twice the length of the arrow, or more exactly one's draw length. Herrin added the .14 for a safety margin.

The Cherokee bow also differs from the Algonkian in that the limbs taper from a 1$\frac{1}{2}$-inch width at the handle area to about one inch at the nock ends. Another uniform feature of the Cherokee bow is the diamond-shaped limb tips and nock formation. The choice wood for the eastern Cherokee was black locust, but hickory was also desirable. For later Cherokees, forced west into Oklahoma, osage became the best choice.

An alternate Cherokee style incorporates a rigid handle formation. This bow is usually a little longer to compensate for the non-working handle. It is preferred by contemporary western Cherokees because it shoots somewhat sweeter by avoiding the tendency for hand shock in the D-type version.

Toxophilites owe a great deal of thanks to Al Herrin's work and for sharing his knowledge of Cherokee archery. Herrin is a bowyer, hunter, and scholar

(Ph.D. in American Culture)—a model of the values of traditional archery, and a champion of his people. He writes a regular column in *Traditional Bowhunter Magazine*, publishes an independent newsletter, and is the author of *Cherokee Bows and Arrows: How to Make and Shoot Primitive Bows and Arrows*. This book, as far as I know, is the only Native American archery book focused on one group and written by a member of that group (with full Cherokee ancestry).

Wampanoag (or Sudbury) Bow

This is probably the type of bow the Plymouth Colony settlers saw when they landed in the new world. This example was collected from a Wampanoag who was shot by one of the settlers in the village of Sudbury, Massachusetts, in 1660. Now the bow resides in the Peabody Museum at Harvard. It is 67 inches long, $1^{7}\!/\!8$ inches wide at the widest portion of the limbs, tapering to about $3\!/\!4$ inch at the ends. The tips are about $3\!/\!8$ inch thick.

Wampanoag (or Sudbury) is probably the most basic model for American, self-, and flatbows, and are another great contribution of the Native Americans.

There is no way of knowing which of the Woodland bows came first, or which group may have influenced another, but this bow may indicate an evolution—one more step in refining the design of the Cherokee handled bow. These two bows are very similar in many respects, with the exception of more marked tapering from the handle to the widest part of the limb, and more pronounced tapering from there to the limb tip. The limb of the Wampanoag is $1\!/\!4$ inch narrower than the Cherokee at the nock point, and the Wampanoag limb is $1\!/\!4$ inch wider at its widest point (mid-limb) than the Cherokee. The cross section is similar to the Cherokee; however, the edges are sloped such that the belly is wider than the back.

In terms of widespread knowledge of Native American bows, this model is one of the better known, and I believe the most widely reproduced by self-bow makers. Modern versions usually have more rounded edges and other modifications on the exact shape of the cross section.

The engineering savvy of utilizing so widely the flat limb structure attests to the intelligence and inventiveness of the Native Americans. The efficiency and durability of this basic flat design has been corroborated by the well known and rigorous scientific tests of physicist, bowyer, and archer Paul Klopsteg. The design and art of the Woodland bow live on with integrity, while the inaccurate and uncharitable social conceptions of the Colonists have been cast aside.

Penobscot Bows

Penobscot Bay lies about mid-point on the coast of Maine. Legend has it that the Penobscot Indians searched for a bow design that had greater cast and would reach far enough into the bay to shoot flaming arrows into the ships of the European invaders. While they may or may not have achieved their goal in the most efficient way, the concept is a *tour de force* of experimentation and product development.

The concept calls for a traditional long bow of a flat-limbed design. To this basic full-sized bow, a much smaller bow, about half the length, is lashed to the back. When the combined bows are pulled as a unit, the extra kinetic energy stored in the small bow combines with the energy stored in the larger bow. The physics, however, supposedly do not indicate a proportionate increase in draw weight. Thus, an additional bonus cast is added for any given draw weight. The Penobscot form has a half-dozen variations.

Its dimensions are so numerous that they will not be included here. I know several archers who hunt with a Penobscot and have myself shot two different variations. They are smooth, accurate, and comfortable; the unusually large handle mass undoubtedly

The Choctaw bow has an elegant dot and semi-circle decorative pattern by Rob Young of Idaho.

Amazing Penobscot double bow by Judson Bailey.

adds to performance stability. Very few bowyers have attempted to re-create the Penobscot, as tillering the two bows simultaneously (getting a smooth gradual bend when drawn) is very difficult. Judson Bailey in Maine has pioneered the research and the re-creation of these bows, however. His demanding engineering standards and superb crafting skills necessary for his extremely costly customized rifles carry over into his Penobscot craft.

Plains Bows

The tall straight knot-free timber common for the eastern Woodlands was non-existent or at least very rare on the open plains. During the pre-horse days, Plains Indians apparently traded either for staves or for ready-made bows with sources in the Rocky Mountain region. Hamm (Ed., 1994) describes two Plains bows discovered in arid areas of Texas, one from a grave and another from a cave. One is a very long bow (75 inches) resembling the Meare Heath, and the other is a 57-inch round cross section with a set back handle and limbs with pronounced string follow—both imports from more western sites.

The Coming of the Horse

The horse did not exist in North America until it was introduced by the Spanish in the early 1600s. The horse entered the U.S. through the Spanish stock-raising settlements in the Santa Fe area of New Mexico. The southern Plains Indians, such as the Kiowa and the Apache, were using the horse by about 1650, but it took approximately a century before horse culture spread to the northern tribes such as the North Blackfoot, Flatheads, Piegans, and the Mandans and Hidatsa.

We can view the time frame for horse culture as intertwined with that of the buffalo. If the buffalo became scarce by 1875 (and nearly extinct by 1890), for instance, it means that the southern Indians had just over two centuries for the horse/buffalo culture to appear and disappear, while the northern tribes had it for a little over a century. Of course, the Plains Indians hunted the buffalo on foot before the horse, and the horse continued to be used after the buffalo disappeared.

The Horse Bow

Two hundred years, for southern Plains Indians, and even less for the northern tribes, is not much time to develop a fundamentally different kind of bow and its accoutrements. In light of the evidence, however, we must once again admire the intelligence, adaptability, and inventiveness of the Native Americans.

Horsebows were either heavily sinewed wood bows or horn bows. The sinewed-back wood bows ranged from 40 to 55 inches long and were a continuation of the pre-horse days when hunting and warfare were conducted on foot. The pressure to shorten the bow may have been necessary for the close encounter of warfare rather than for the buffalo chase. While the buffalo hunt demanded incredible skill and courage, maneuverability, such as shooting under the horse's neck during battle, may have provided greater impetus for shortening the bow. At any rate, the partial shift to a shorter bow, and heavier reliance on sinew backing was coupled with a shorter draw of 20 to 25 inches. T.M. Hamilton (1982) reminds us that longer bows were often used, accommodating a full 28 to 30-inch draw, and that some of these longer bows may actually have been horn bows.

The Plains horn bow was unique in that it had no wood core, just horn in the belly and sinew forming the back, approximately at a 1:1 proportion. Elkhorn and mountain sheep horn were used with great success. These ranged quite a bit in length, but are commonly found between 33 and 40 inches with some reaching 50 inches. Cast and penetration were enhanced by the horn. At close range in a buffalo chase, these bows could drive an arrow into the vital heart and lung area. Often more than one arrow was required, yet a kill from a single arrow was not uncommon. Sometimes an arrow even penetrated clear through the animal.

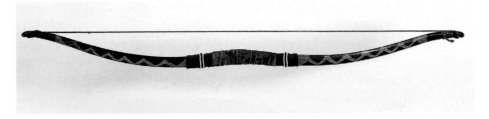

Western Plains hornbow with beautiful handle treatment, limb painting, and heavily sinewed limb tip treatment by David Kissinger of Gaines, Pennsylvania.

Any horn bow requires a much broader repertoire of knowledge, skill, and time than the self– or sinew-backed bow. High quality horn is often difficult to find, and the time invested for construction is great—often months of drying time must pass between applying layers of sinew. All this adds up to an expensive bow. The horn bow of yesteryear, as well as today's re-creation, is the Cadillac of the bow. Economics dictate that not every hunter or warrior goes to the field with a hornbow in hand. Many of the Plains people undoubtedly used the sinew-backed version.

The Buffalo Hunt

The chase is on. Imagine that you have picked your animal and after a furious chase you are closing ranks on the right side of the beast. You are choking, struggling to see through the clouds of dust, deafened by the thundering hoofs of the one-ton beast and dozens of other tightly clustered bison. Your pony is a heaving and straining inferno under you, unleashing every ounce of speed possible. Bison calves stumble and roll about in the dust. Your target throws his furious head and heavy horns at you, nearly skewering you and your pony. Froth flies from his nostrils out into the air. When the moment arrives, you settle in position and release the arrow. With lightning speed, a second arrow leaps from your bow hand, sinking into its vitals for good measure. Sure of your hits, you pull a little away from the animal for safety. After a few gasping paces, the great bison stumbles and goes down. Pandemonium over, your pulse slows. Soon the butchering will begin, the process of harvesting the precious material that will feed and clothe your family.

But what came before the chase, before the bow's creation and the years of practicing with it? Not just any horse can run the buffalo, the danger is as palpable to the horse as to the rider. It takes a horse of great courage and speed, tempered with a steady disposition and responsiveness, to take cues given from the rider's legs. The chase unfolds without reins; both hands are fully engaged with the shooting. So horses used during the buffalo chase were developed through selective breeding. They were tested under stress, and finally trained over long periods of horse and archer working as one. The buffalo-chase horse was used for nothing else.

West Coastal Bows

The family of coastal bows tends to have a set of common characteristics. They are usually short, wide, thin, and highly decorated, yet even within those typical features there are significant variations. These bows are as short as thirty inches and as long as the mid-50s, and average 35 to 45 inches. There is usually a marked handle of about $1^{1}/2$ inches in width, with the limbs flaring out to 2 to $2^{1}/2$ inches or even three inches. The limbs are relatively very thin, perhaps only $5/16$ inch or $5/8$ inch at mid-limb. The limb cross-sections are flattened ovals with somewhat sharpened edges, and are thus lenticular. Because of the extremely wide shape of the limbs, these weapons are sometimes referred to as "paddle bows."

Coastal bows are often recurved, sinew backed, and the sinew-backed types are deeply reflexed when unstrung. The longer non-sinewed bows may have been used in very damp weather, which may play some havoc with sinew-backed bows unless they are well waterproofed.

The other striking feature of these bows is that they are frequently decorated with elaborate geometric designs. Compared to the subdued decorations of the Woodland bow, the Coastal bow is far more colorful, intricate, and elaborate. Remember that the original paintings were pre-acrylic; they were all made from natural dyes. Each color dye often took many steps to prepare— pulverizing, heating, grinding, straining, re-drying, and mixing with other bases and glues. Finding four to six different colors on one bow is not unusual.

What propelled the Hupa, Karoks, Modocs, and other coastal people to develop the paddle-like design of the limbs, and what led them to their elaborate

West Coast bows by Rob Young. Left to right, a Hupa, Karok, three Modacs, and a Chinook.

decorations? We do not know. It may have been their particular avenue of cultural conformity, providing them a sense of identity and belonging. The wider limb surfaces may have presented too inviting a canvas. Whatever the original motivation may have been, the aesthetic beauty should be easy to appreciate for any observer. Many of these bows were made from yew, a wood that lends itself to many different sound structural designs. Getting to the good yew in the Cascades, however, may have been an obstacle. So, the wide use and availability of cedar, juniper, and other conifers may explain the wide, thin limb solution which spreads the compression stress over a wide area in the belly and, likewise, the tension stress on the back. Sinewing also makes sense under these conditions, and the shortened limbs would be necessary for a reasonable cast.

While functionality is at the heart of the bow, its beauty is not just skin deep. Across the continent, these were a people of fashion. The elaborate variations of the males' ceremonial headdresses, and intricacy of the total costume—down to the moccasins, the quillwork, beadwork, and metal and bone accents—all advertise high fashion. Compare the Metropolitan Museum's print of the Bodmer painting in which a Moennitarri warrior from the Hidatsa Tribe is performing the Dog Dance ritual. The balance of refinement and boldness from the headdress through the total costume is hard to miss.

Far Northern Bows

In the far North the choice of wood was very limited, although it's not as marked in southern Alaska.

On the Alaskan Peninsula, the Koniag could gather ample softwoods and even some hardwoods. The red and black decorated Koniag shown is a 45-inch, rawhide backed hickory bow. Caribou and otters are painted on the back, depicting the use of the bow in both land and sea hunting. It has a concave back and is made for the shorter 25-inch draw.

The Aleut also hail from the Alaskan Peninsula. The replication pictured here is by Doug Theiner of Alaska. This hickory bow is 45 inches long, with a sinewed back, and artificial sinew cabling. The original, of course, would have been entirely cabled with genuine sinew.

The Inuit, and any other groups living in these frozen and barren environments, were hard-pressed to acquire wood of any type, let alone of high quality. As a result, they became masters of the cabling technique. One or more uniform cables of neatly twisted sinew run the full length of their bows with periodic half-hitches of the same cable circling the limb every so often. In places of particular stress, the loops of sinew encircling the limb form a solid covering of sinew, packed tightly side by side. It is easy to see how these cable applications enhance tensile or tension strength on the back of the bow, but how it helps resist the compression dynamics in the belly of the bow is less clear.

Very detailed drawings of many of the varied cabling patterns are still available in O.T. Mason and G. Fowke's (1995)

Alaskan Aleut bow with cabling on the back and geometric land and sea animal paintings by Doug Theiner.

**Alaskan Koniag, deep red with black designs
by Doug Theiner.**

collection of reports and drawings for the Smithsonian between 1889 and 1893 (see the 1995 reprint). The meticulous
application of the cables indicates both the strength and the
beauty of the technique. As to performance, a north
Alaskan Eskimo group, the Chukchi, claimed they could
split a blade of grass with their bows; hopefully it was a
wide blade.

Two unusual "Eskimo" bow configurations deserve
some comment. One commonly found in many museums,
is made up of three curved bows: a major bow about
twenty-four inches long with the handle in the middle, and
two smaller bows, or curves, each about 11 inches long fin-
ishing out the top and bottom limbs. Pronounced elbows
appear in both limbs where the smaller bows meet the
larger one. From the side, the effect is like that of a Mongol
bow, with lines as in a bow with siyahs. In fact, the Mason
report refers to this structure as Tatar (Mason , 1995 reprint,
plate LXVII).

In the subsequent plate we see a similar form. The side
view, unstrung, definitely seems to have siyahs. The limb
has an abrupt reflex about eight inches from the tip and
forms a straight line from the elbow to the very tip. Unfortunately, there is no front or back view to reveal whether or
not the limb narrows abruptly from that viewpoint as a
siyah does. Surely, the idea of a siyah did not exist on the
Siberian side before the ice-bridge migration; at that early
date the bow had probably not even been invented yet. It
makes one wonder if there had been some travel across the
Bering Strait during the centuries of bow development. Yet
the simultaneous invention in different parts of the world
of the siyah-like structure is possible.

Current North America

Currently, some of the best North American bows are replications of Native American bows. However, it is common knowledge that the bow had faded into obscurity in the United States in the middle of the 1800s. Its revival came from two sources—the English longbow tradition, and the tiny scattered remnants of tribes such as the Yani in California and the Cherokee who clung to its use.

After the Civil War, firearms possession was very restricted in the South. Archery, however, was permitted, and it soon became the hunting and sporting outlet for two brothers who were to play a pivotal role in the revival of archery—Maurice (pronounced Morris) and Will Thompson. Their bow of choice was the English longbow, the one most readily available, although by import, and their interest led Maurice to write *The Witchery of Archery,* which was published 1878. His book hastened the interest in archery both on the course and in the hunt. Only a year after the first edition, an archery association had been formed, and the first tournament was held that summer in Chicago.

In the first half of the twentieth century Saxton Pope and Art Young were also shooting the English longbow, striking at the gold of the target and at big game. Nevertheless they were influenced by the American Indian tradition of the flatbow and their association with Ishi, the Yana Indian. This influence predominates to this very day in many modern variations. This family of flat-limbed bows came to be called the American Longbow.

The Self Flatbow

The flattened limb of the bows of the east and west coast Native Americans was like a magnet to the primitive or very traditional bowyer. Made from one piece of wood, this bow more often than not most closely resembles the Wampanoag (Sudbury) model. I first had the pleasure of shooting a Wampanoag bow with my son on one of the 3-D courses at the Eastern Traditional Archery Rendezvous in 1998. It was comfortable, and exciting, and I shot respectably for my first time. In the hands of an expert archer, however, it would have been smashing.

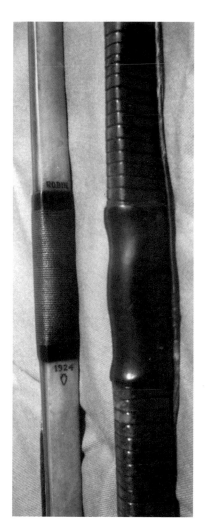

Saxton Pope's "Robin" bow handle on left, and Art Young's "Simba" handle on right, used on lion hunts in Africa. Courtesy of the St. Charles Museum in Seattle, Washington.

Laminated Bows (the Sugarcreek)

Gluing two or more bow-length pieces of wood together for greater strength was not unknown to the ancients of northern Europe or the Asian steppes. Some of the Native Americans used lamination techniques, but the practice was very limited. The early style of the laminated bow highlighted here is the Sugarcreek Natural, designed jointly by the author and Tim Troyer, and refined by Gregg Coffey. The goal was to capture some of the spirit of the 1920s and 30s in a simple two or three lamination bow, emphasizing dramatic natural contrasting wood colors combined with good performance. It was inspired by the bows of John Grumley and Fred Bear, and it has a deep belly of osage with a thin hickory backing and a maple core. This white, tan, and yellow (hickory, maple, and osage) combination is set off with a very dark wenge handle riser wrapped in newbuck leather and wenge static recurved tips, with brush nocks set between the hickory and osage lams by using a deep and very visible "V" joint. The result, after much trial and error, is a smooth performing, crisp casting, and, we think, absolutely beautiful creation. I shot it on a 3-D course at the Great Lakes Longbow Invitational in the summer of 2000 with an excellent archer and hunter, and I was very pleased. The Sugarcreek was matched against a Hummingbird, one of the finest contemporary longbows that has the advantage of an arrow shelf and window, and fiberglass reinforcement.

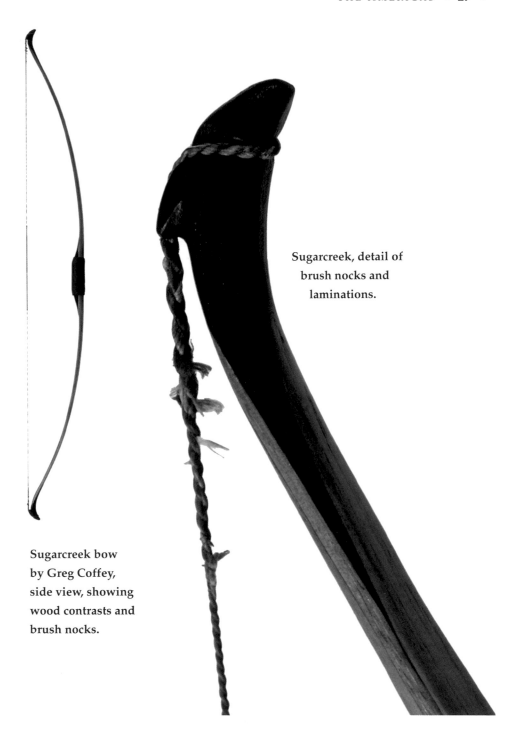

Sugarcreek, detail of brush nocks and laminations.

Sugarcreek bow by Greg Coffey, side view, showing wood contrasts and brush nocks.

Laminated Glass-backed Longbows

The practice of applying a layer of fiberglass to the back and the belly of a bow consisting of two or more wood laminations became a common practice in the 1950s. The Hill style bow was a leader; unstrung, the back of the bow formed a straight line. The more modern versions have widely adopted the deflex-reflex line when unstrung. The handle area curves inward toward the archer (deflex) and the outer limbs curve away from the archer (reflex). The Kentuckian by Roy McIntosh and the Regent-K by Fritz Jonck are shown here, but there are many other fine makers of this type of bow. The Kentuckian exemplifies simple elegance—fewer lams with harmonious coloring and non-exotic riser and handle construction. The Regent exhibits six lams of highly contrasting colors, and intricate joinery of several exotic woods in the riser. There are three redheart wood diamonds set into each of the Regent's limbs. Both examples have

Longbow by Roy McIntosh of Kentuckian Longbows.

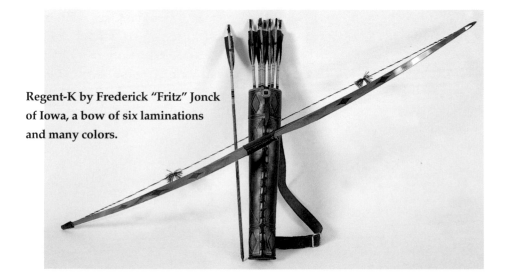

Regent-K by Frederick "Fritz" Jonck of Iowa, a bow of six laminations and many colors.

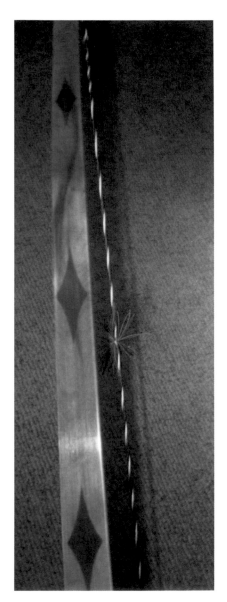

Regent-K details, diamonds on back set in a swirled yew backing.

superbly smooth and flawless finishes and joinery, and excellent performance.

The rebirth of traditional archery has also spawned a rich array of quiver makers and arrow smiths around the world. The quiver matching the decor of the Regent bow by Larry Snell of Classic Quivers, is typical of the best quiver makers' artistry.

The Glass-backed Recurve

The modern recurve developed parallel with the modern longbow. Bear, Wing, Shakespeare and other companies began producing recurves in small-scale factory production. My first adult bow was a Bear Kodiak Hunter. In the early 1970s, my wife had hidden it under the Christmas tree, and it has been a great delight all along. I have also purchased wonderful second-hand versions of this bow for my three sons-in-law with good effect each time. The modern example shown here is made by Roy Hall of Navajo Longbows.

Takedown recurve named "Navajo II" by Roy Hall. The limbs come off for easy traveling and hunting trips.

The All-wood Preference

While fiberglass and carbon construction is here to stay, providing powerful and durable weapons, some prefer the softer feel of drawing all-wood bows. A very high level of performance, coupled with unique artistic achievement, is celebrated by the Oak Leaf Bow of Brad Smith. It is a self-bow of osage with rawhide backing for a better painting surface—an opportunity that was not passed up, as it is expertly painted in an oak leaf motif with obscure turkey and deer interspersed. The tips have English-like nocks, and the cross section is a moderately flattened "D" section. It has a small arrow shelf and is exceptionally easy in regard to achieving accuracy.

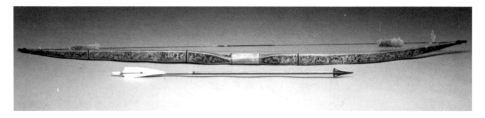

Oak Leaf self longbow by bowyer, hunter, artist and musician, Brad Smith.

Bamboo has also become increasingly popular. The modern bamboo-faced bows of Lukas Novotny of Saluki Bows demonstrates this trend at its best. Very careful selection and preparation of bamboo, combined with excellent workmanship and constant field testing, give us another extremely attractive and efficient option.

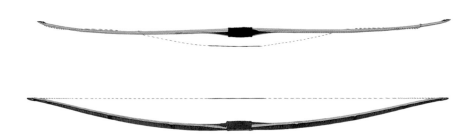

Excellent examples of bamboo back and belly bows by Lukas Novotny of Saluki Bows in Ohio.

South America

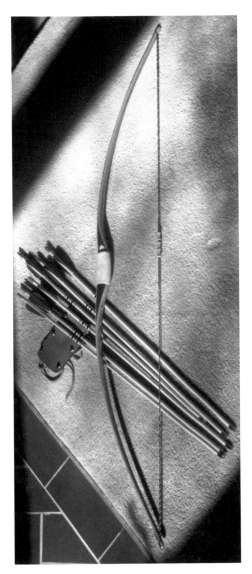

Skipping over Mexico and Central America, which deserve a book of their own, let us get at least a meager sampling of the archery achievements from South America. We'll focus on the greater Amazon Basin, which makes up about one-third of the whole continent. Most of the study of archery has been done here.

The paucity of our knowledge concerning South American archery, and of the South American culture in general, is undoubtedly a result of our exploitation of that continent. Plundering for silver and gold, then coffee, bananas, and minerals, and today, for oil and tropical wood—not to mention a constant source of cheap labor—has blinded us to the riches of this continent's native cultures.

The bows shown in this section are from tribes in northern and southern Venezuela. Although guns have penetrated the rain forest tribes, the bow and arrow are still affordable and quiet, and are therefore still widely used, and many hunters are deadly shots. Early in these cultures,

Child bow, "Mighty Hunter" by Kentuckian Longbows. All of the quality and polish of the nicest of adult bows.

labor was sharply divided, a split often referred to as "the bow and the basket" divide. If a man was made to hunt, he trained for this task as a child. When he became too old to hunt, and had to help gather with a basket, he was no longer considered a man. The point here is not sexist but to explain how important the bow was. When a man died, his bow was burned. When a woman died, her basket was burned. The tools and the genders that used them were intertwined; one could not go on without the other.

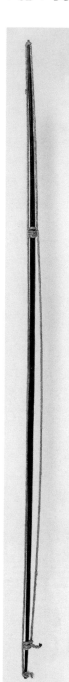

A jittery, jumping monkey 90 feet up a tree in a dense forest is not an easy target. Birds on wing or wild hogs in dense undergrowth are not for the timid or average shooter. Likewise, the uncanny and swift movements of fish in a rapid current present a supreme challenge to the indigenous archer. After all, this is the only supermarket in town. If you don't know how to shop, there's no way to bring home the bacon—or fish. Every expert hunter comes home empty handed much of the time, but not these people.

What's the secret to their success? Wand shooting. It underlines the skill of these jungle archers. Although a target could be a narrow stake an inch or two wide, and they may be at a range of 50 or more yards, their high saturation of hits in wand shooting will earn the admiration and respect of any spectator who is able to appreciate the difficulty of traditional archery.

The Bari Bow

This bow is a very long 70 inches, and is made of a dense, hard, and heavy palm wood (mancanilla in Spanish). It pulls about 50 pounds at a 25-inch draw and is about $1^{3}/16$ inches wide and $^{5}/8$ inch thick at the handle, tapering to $^{5}/8$ inch at the tips. The cross section is oval-shaped at the handle area, and round at the ends of the limbs. The string is made from bromelia fibers and is nearly a quarter-inch thick. An extra string is attached to the bow, and it is only braced to about an inch.

The Yanomami Bow

From the much-publicized tribe in the southern edge of the Venezuelan rainforest, this bow is made from a similar hard

Bari bow from Venezuela in the Amazonian River Basin.
Note their technique for carrying an extra string.

palm wood, called Seje of Hoko. It is very similar to the Bari bow except that the cross sections are almost round throughout. The limbs are evenly and smoothly tapered to a blunt point about $\frac{1}{2}$ inch in diameter at the tip. The natural fiber string is about $\frac{1}{8}$ inch thick and is made from the inner bark of a ficus-like tree in the fig family. If taken to a temperate climate, these bows will dry out. To remain functional, they must be immersed in water.

Arrows that typically go with these bows are generally as long as the bows—only the tips differ, depending on the use. The reason for the arrow's extreme length may be to aid in retrieval both in the dense rainforest and in shallow lake and stream fishing (no bow line or reel is used).

Yanomami bow. Counter to traditional archery wisdom, the six-foot-long reed arrows shot from these bows are accurate and deadly at thirty yards.

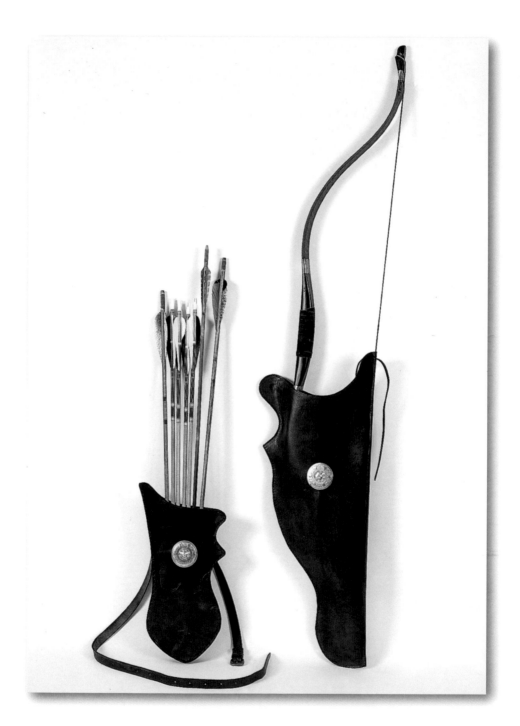

Polish military bow by Polish bowyer Jan Bisok.

3 · Europe

"**And** in his hand he held a mighty bow." This quote is from *Toxophilus* by Roger Ascham, 1545. For many it conjures up the visage of the strong Yeomen of Agincourt and Crecy—mighty archers who pulled the Mary Rose war bows. The legends of Sherwood Forest, the actual archery performance of King Henry VIII, the shooting of Horace Ford, and the very late towering influence of Richard Galloway have all left their stamp on archers everywhere. The many impressive older shooting societies of England and Scotland, and the vital and widespread practice of "shooting in the longbow" today, testify to the stature of the English Longbow. It is apparently a mistake, however, to think that the longbow had a monopoly on bow designs in the post-Renaissance period. The all-wood recurve type of bow was also common across most of Europe and the Isles. Chris Boyton, who apprenticed under Richard Galloway, and Hilary Greenland are two respected English bowyers that attest to the substantial presence of the recurve.

The English Longbow

The English inherited the basics of the longbow from ancient bowyers as outlined in the chapter on prehistoric bows. The superiority of yew wood was not a new idea, nor was the basic "D" cross section. Even its relatively long length was not new. Stiffening the handle section to reduce hand shock is a 9,000-year-old practice. So why is it the *English* Longbow? Perhaps for several reasons. The English fighting forces used the bow to its full advantage in battle, especially in terms of the number of archers who could employ special tactics such as the rain of arrows, and specialized arrow heads that were used for different purposes. In addition to this deadly force, the English bowyers added improvements. One enhancement was the reinforcement of the horn tip, which allowed limb tips to be more tapered, so they were lowered in mass and as a result had better cast. The padded handle grip, added much later during the Victorian era, made shooting easier, and once strike plates were attached, wear to the side of the bow was reduced, and its overall beauty was enhanced. As an added plus, the arrow shelf/window has always been verboten in the genuine English design.

Finally, the people of the Isles sustained the longbow practice for pleasure and self-improvement in a relatively unbroken stream long after warring days had ceased. Taken together, all of these elements ensured the longbow's status in the history books.

While ancient bowyers found the yew tree produced a superior bow, they usually cut from its center rather than using a stave from the perimeter. The English bowyers, and maybe others before them, split their staves from the outer edge of the tree. The softer sap-wood is usually considered inferior for woodworking purposes, but in the yew the sapwood provides the natural tensile or tension strength needed for stretching the fibers in the back of the bow. On the other hand, the heartwood of the yew withstands the compression on the belly of the bow, as the fibers crunch or compact in the drawn bow. As a gift of nature, then, the yew bow achieves the dual tension/compression ideal of well-selected and crafted laminations. One can easily see the phenomenon of something like natural lamination in the side view of a yew self-bow, because the sapwood is light in color and the heartwood is darker. High quality yew was often expensive and difficult to get, however, so laminated bows often used dagame (lemon wood) or lacewood in the belly and hickory on the back.

It may be that the English were responsible for lengthening the bow, and certainly for experimenting with many cross section variations. H. D. Soar (1994) outlines at least six different variations on the "D" cross section. The flat part of the "D" on the Mary Rose warbow was rounded on the back so that the section was basically a circle, and the height of the stack, or camber, was varied, resulting in either a deep or slightly flattened "D." I do not know of any controlled comparative studies of the relative efficiencies of these variations.

A Muir Longbow Survivor

My son-in-law was fortunate enough to retrieve a Muir longbow from a rare bookstore in New England, and then present it to me as a Christmas gift. It had previously been stored in the attic of an old home along with a much lighter woman's longbow and a child's longbow. The Muirs were well-known bowyers in Scotland; "Muir, Edinburgh" is stamped below the handle, and "52" (poundage) is stamped above it. Tip to tip, it's 73 inches, and nock to nock it's 70 inches. The handle width is $1^3/16$ inches, tapering to $1/2$ inch once it enters the black horn tips.

It's self yew with no backing whatsoever; the wood is in immaculate condition, repolished to a silken finish. The heartwood has darkened markedly, as has the sapwood, but the demarcation is still evident between the two. The horn nocks are in nice condition, although each has a crack, and one has a small chip out of it. A right-handed archer often shot the bow, as indicated by the arrow impression worn over the handle; there is no arrow plate. Soar (1995) shows drawings of a Peter or David Muir bow with identical handle and nock treatments from around 1830. Soar claims that Muir's Scottish bows were unsurpassed by the very best English bows. Peter Muir was also a superb archer: the National Champion of Great Britain in 1845, 1847, and 1863, as

English longbow by one of the accomplished Muir Scottish bowyers, about 1850.

Limb tip detail of the old Muir longbow.

handle detail, old Muir longbow.

well as the Scottish National Champion in 1853. The fine condition of the bow suggests that the owner must have loved it as much as I do. Even the handle cover is in fair condition, and the green velvet is intact. The red banding at the handle edges, however, shows age and wear.

Richard Head Longbows

Richard and his son Phillip are two of the many fine bowyers still crafting great English longbows. They make yew self-bows, hickory-backed yew or hickory-backed lemonwood, and tri-laminates. Their tri-laminate bow, featured here, is hickory-backed, with a purple heart core and a lemonwood belly. The bow was made to fit a tall, long-armed archer such as myself, so it's 78 inches tip to tip. The overall configuration is nearly identical to the old Muir described above. The sharply contrasting wood colors are quite dramatic, and the exotic bright red braid handle, trimmed with bands of leather stamped with gold leaf, enhances the flair. It is stamped in the English fashion, 55, 29, that is: 55 pounds at 29 inches. There are also attractive mother of pearl striker plates on both sides of the bow.

A tri-laminate English longbow by Richard Head of Wiltshire, England.

Welchman Longbows

Ironically, two of the English bows on these pages are made in the United States by American bowyers. If there is a certain fascination among Europeans about Native Americans, then Americans enjoy a similar fascination about the English longbow. Another factor of this interest is that some of the best yew available today grows in the Cascade Range in Oregon.

Welchman handle detail.

**Welchman longbow
in the English style by
Gerald Welch of Alaska.**

Gerald Welch periodically travels to the Cascades to cut his own yew, although he lives and works in a remote corner of Alaska. This is a one-piece, yew self-bow with rawhide backing to help protect the soft sapwood. The fine leather wrapping on the handle has continuously tapered edges that have a suave, elegant, and powerful effect.

Pacific Yew

Among the legends of the revival of traditional archery in the United States is the St. Charles family, particularly the senior, Glenn—one of the few living contemporaries of Saxton Pope, Arthur Young, Howard Hill, Fred Bear, and many others. Founder of the Pope and Young Club, he continues to write, speak, and promote the great fellowship of archers. At the Pope and Young Museum in Seattle, one can still find two great old English-style longbows. The 70-pound "Robin" was a favorite of Saxton Pope, and the 70-pound "Simba Blood" was an old trustworthy for Art Young when the two stalked the lions of Africa. These bows are pictured in the previous chapter on North America.

One of Glenn's sons, Jay, owns and operates the "Pacific Yew." The rich tradition of the longbow, borrowed from England, and tried and tested on big and small game around the world, lives on in the many fine variations of yew selfbows and laminates crafted by Jay.

Swiss 1800

This wonderful specimen is patterned after a bow thought to date to the 1800s, but its type goes back as far as the 1500s. The original resides in the Abbey of the Bows in Lausanne, Switzerland. Chris Boyton examined the bow personally at the Abbey and then made this re-creation. Made of billets to get a four-inch backset, the wood is a very rare French timber called liburnum. It is like yew in the sense that the sapwood is used for the back, but the belly of inner wood is much darker than yew, even when freshly worked. The cross section is a moderately bulbous ellipse. A Renaissance German bow in the National Museum in Nuremberg, Germany looks extremely similar (Riesch, 1995).

Chris field-tested the bow at a local shoot and took first prize. I personally picked it up, with pleasure, from Chris on the way home from a meeting in Poland. It was a great honor to meet him and his family, and to have a living touch, as it were, with the master English bowyers.

Swiss 1800, a mighty one-of-kind longbow by Chris Boyton of Middlesex, England.

Now, however, the bow belongs to Norman Graham, a United States Olympic Committee member, and I keep hoping the Olympics will institute a bare-bow class competition. It's intriguing to look at old pictures of the first international archery tournament held in Poland in 1931. All the bows are English bare longbows. We can also see a Polish archery couple, and the woman's bow is about a foot taller than she, and the man's is about eight inches taller. These were the embryonic days of the Federation of International Target Archery (FITA).

The Olympic high-tech Recurve and Compound classes are both fine, high-level, and ultimately demanding competitions. Those classes deserve the respect of all archers. Rod White, one of the three American team winners at Atlanta in 1996, grew up and trained at a Junior Olympic range just ten miles away from my home in western Pennsylvania. He shoots in the Recurve Class with balances, sights, and a tab release. His picture hangs on my wall, because I am so proud of his accomplishment. When he was twelve, Rod started to "robin hood" his arrows (shooting one arrow into another), and hurried home to tell his Dad, "I am determined to go to the Olympics." That deep grit, coupled with a humane patience, is a great model for young people today.

The Renaissance Longbow

This modern bow, shown at right, is inspired by the bows used by the Italian armies of the fourteenth and fifteenth centuries. A setback handle with re-curved limbs was a popular design of this period, even appearing in many Italian art works. A fresco near Florence, in fact, depicts the Martyrdom of

St. Sebastian with an archer bracing a bow of this design. Sketches by Leonardo da Vinci from the late 1400s also portray the setback handle and recurved limbs. Currently, the bow has been documented by Alessio Cenni, and is being made by Hilary Greenland in England. Cenni describes these bows as "lightly recurved" (Cenni, 1997). Greenland chooses to name it as she has, because it is 70 inches long to accommodate a 28-inch draw. The reader should be alerted, however, that many versions of recurves and straight longbows were in vogue in these early years in Italy and throughout the continent. The Italian armies of this period may not have relied on the bow as a primary weapon, but military archers were apparently valued more than many of the other European forces.

The J,Uhu, or Owl Bow (Greenhorn)

This bow is a conglomeration of materials, unusual history, and time periods. It is a take-down. The sleeve handle take-down mechanism was patented in both Sweden and the United States as early as 1927. It is a glass-backed bow, yet it retains the old horn-nock features. A brass plate encircles the entire bow at the top of the handle, forming an arrow shelf for left- or right-handed shooters. Attractive gold stamped braid bands set off the top and bottom of the handsome black leather handle. The lams are made up of dagame, greenheart, and fancywood. It is 68 inches long and comes either in an overall black or white facing. Fast flight string is added to the seemingly incongruous but most attractive mix of elements.

Polish Bows

The Polish Lithuanian Commonwealth towered in size and military prowess in the 1600s, yet greatest of all was its tolerance, diversity, love of freedom, and democratic/republic form of government. It was clearly the earliest, biggest, and longest lasting democracy in Europe. In light of the great prowess and civilization of the Polish-Lithuanian Commonwealth in the 1600s and early 1700s, one would expect the Polish bowyers to have left some unique stamp on the bows of that age. But this does not seem to be the case. The bows, arrows, and quivers documented by Jerzy Werner (1974) suggest that the Poles merely adopted and perfected the use of the Turkish bow (See Page 34).

The European Legacy

The legacy of archery from this part of the world is indeed impressive. The longbow in its many variations of stacked and flat limbs descends from antiquity. And the military longbow was astutely used primarily by the British in the medieval wars. The renowned shooting societies, including the highest of nobility, leave an indelible trail of achievement and interest. Current target and field archery is clearly vital, with many expert bowyers and champion archers practicing, not to mention the respected archery magazines of England, France, Germany, and Hungary. Finally, the museums of Europe hold some of the world's most extensive and coveted collections of archery treasures from around the world.

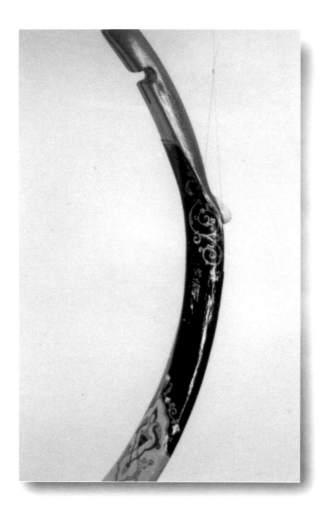

Turkish-type siyah, bow by Lukas Novotny.

4 · Asia

In the 1100s and 1200s, the Mongol Empire became one of the largest empires in ancient or modern history. Their mounted archer bands struck their enemies unexpectedly with lightning speed, delivering a deadly barrage of arrows and disappearing before any possible counterattack. A second attack would come from a different direction with the same lethal force, or a feigned retreat would draw the heavy and slower horses of the armored cavalry close enough to ensure parting shots through armor seams or to trample the knights by tumbling their horses to their deaths. The Asian horn bows and the skilled mounted archers that used them played center stage in this chapter in history.

The culture of the horse archer had been fermenting for a very long time before the Mongols appeared. The cultural brew had been in the making for about a thousand years in one version or another. The Greek writer of the classic *Odyssey* and the *Iliad* wrote about a Scythian people who were "horsemilkers" and "horsearchers." Although they were a nomadic people, they had a settled base on the north shore of the Black Sea. But they held nomadic dominion over the great plains, or steppes, reaching as far east as modern day Mongolia. The Scythian impact on eastern Europe was followed by the Huns in 300 and 400 A.D. The Avars came into the Carpathian Basin between 600 and 800 A.D., and finally Magyars came to claim what we now know as Hungary in a conquest dated 896 A.D.

In the larger Asian picture, the variety of bow designs, unique and varied styles of shooting, and the broad range of approaches to the inner game of archery, make Asia one of the world's greatest treasure chests. Its depth and breadth match the vastness and diversity of the huge continent itself.

For those of us in the western world, the closest edge of the Asian archery world is eastern Europe. Bows of the Ukraine, Poland, and Hungary are more clearly Asian than European, so these countries mark Asian archery's western perimeter. The cultural impact of ancient Asian invasions into Europe was generally more profound and lasting in eastern Europe than in western Europe. Archery is no exception. This is not to say that a variety of Asian bows—Scythian, Hun, Avar, Magyar, Mongol, and Indo-Persian—did not infiltrate western Europe, but they never became as predominant as in the East.

Evolution from Self-Bows to Laminated Bows

The earliest and simplest form of the bow in any tradition is the self-bow. One single piece of wood, probably originally a small sapling with its branches removed, had notches cut in its ends to hold the string. In refined and dressed-up versions, the self-bow is reported as a viable option in manuscripts dated near the end of the medieval period (*Arab Archery*, and *Saracen Archery*). These refinements took the form of sophisticated variations on the "flat limb" design, as well as the more stacked-or rounded-limb design.

The self-bow was followed by early forms of lamination, namely two pieces of wood running the full length of the bow. We would guess that the search for wood that could stand up to the strain of compression in the belly, and other wood with good tensile strength for the back of the bow, was under way very early in Asia, at least two millennia B.C. Possibly an earlier motivation for lamination was quite simply overall strength. A weakness or undesirable dynamic in one piece of wood may be complemented or reinforced by stronger or opposing forces in the second piece. At any rate, it seems safe to assume that the compression/tension insight dates back two full millennia B.C. because there is already evidence of composite bows that early.

Apparently looking for an even better performance than lamination provides, entirely new bow making materials were sought. Animal parts such as antler, horn, bone, skin, sinew, gut, and hair were all put to the test. Plant (other than wood) and insect products were also examined, including hemp, linen, silk, woven bark, and plant fibers. Copper, iron, and steel were also given a chance.

The Breakthrough of the Composite Bow

Sometime during the latter part of the third millennium B.C., experimentation with an array of materials led to the combination of three basic bow substances—wood, horn, and sinew. These three have been the touchstone of the composite bow ever since. A composite bow is often referred to just as a horn bow, in which case the use of wood and sinew is understood to be included. The Akkadian cylinder seal of Ibil-Ishtar (c. 2370-2320 B.C.) shows a hunter carrying a short, braced bow, which some believe to be the oldest representation of a composite bow. The development of the composite bow in the Asian regions was probably the first anywhere in the world. The Native North Americans also developed a fine composite bow (without the wood core), but it came many centuries later. For a chronological perspective on this breakthrough in Asian archery, remember that the age of pyramid building also occurred in the middle of the third millennium.

If there is any uncertainty about the early emergence of the composite bow, evidence abounds for a somewhat later date in a plethora of bas-reliefs dated from 1500 to 1200 B.C. Especially striking are the chariot bows of the Egyptians shown at full draw where the bow forms a full half circle. Observing the relative shortness of these bows, combined with the long, deep overdraw, makes it quite certain that these were more than wood self-bows or wood laminates. They almost certainly had to employ horn and sinew.

Why are horn, wood, and sinew such a winning combination? A number of animals (bovine, goat, and especially water buffalo) have ideal horns for the belly of the bow, the side next to the archer. This side must compress together and spring back in order to create the energy for casting the arrow. At the cell level, the horn material must withstand rapidly squeezing and expanding without the cell walls crushing. Where there is a whole "fault line" of crushing in the belly of a wood self-bow, this crushing shows up as a "fault line," which, to the naked eye, looks like a zigzagged diagonal line; this is called crysalling. Horn, however, turns out to be a marvelous spring; the archer pulls the ends of the spring toward each other, and the spring recoils upon release.

On the other hand, the back of the bow, the side facing way from the archer, undergoes opposite demands; it must have enough elasticity to stretch repeatedly. Of all known natural substances, sinew meets these demands best. Sinew is glued onto the back of the bow in thin layers and built up to perhaps a thickness of as much as $1/8$ inch or even $1/4$ inch. This involves a long process: heating and softening the sinew by boiling the tendons of an animal's leg or back, and then hammering them into fine fibers. Thin layers of these fibers are then applied to the back of the bow with glue made from animal hide. In some of the Eastern Asian traditions, drying times between layers of glue may be several weeks or even several months.

A framework of wood sits between the horn belly and the sinew back. In its earliest form, it may have started out as one piece of wood tapered both ways at both ends of the bow, but the wood frame became a much more sophisticated structure. The wood core of the Turkish bow is usually composed of five pieces of wood glued together utilizing deep "V" splices. Some cores use up to nine different pieces of wood. Thus, different kinds of wood can be combined to meet the different needs of the core's portions—rigid wood for limb tips and handles, and more elastic wood for the deep-bending Asian limbs. In addition, the wood pieces can be set at different angles to maximize the dynamics of a particular design—the deep angling or reflexing, for instance, of the limb tips called siyahs.

Adding the Siyah to the Composite Bow

The siyah is the fairly long, static, and rigid end of the limb, actually it's an ending that is attached to the working limb. The siyah, or ear, acts as a lever to help the limb bend into a tighter "spring," which allows that spring to be all the more sturdy in order to increase the subsequent recoil. Siyahs range greatly in length—about $4^{1}/_{2}$ inches, or 11cm, on the short Korean bow to ten inches, or 25cm, on the upper siyah of the longer Hun bow. In this photograph of five Asian bows on the next page, the Korean bow on the right has a blue tip, a red leather string pad-type bridge, and a bronze wrap where the siyah meets the limb. The Hun bow on the left has a tan-colored ash siyah and bright red cord wraps between the siyah and the limbs.

The photograph of the side-by-side siyah comparisons reveals a number of other differences. Not only are the different lengths of the siyahs obvious, but the angle, cant, or reflex away from the string also varies greatly. The siyahs on the Korean bow cant the most, followed by the Hun and then the Mongol. The Mongol, second from the right, has gray-colored limbs. The other two bows are versions of the Magyar. Notice that the string does not ride on or bend around the siyah at all for these two bows.

The third difference, which can be seen in the Korean bow above all others, is the smooth integration of the siyah into the limb. Turkish bows are similar in this respect, which means that Korean and Turkish bows look somewhat like a more modern recurve at first glance. In contrast, the Chinese bow, the North Indian, and the Indo-Persian bows all have very obvious, less integrated siyahs similar to the Mongol bow.

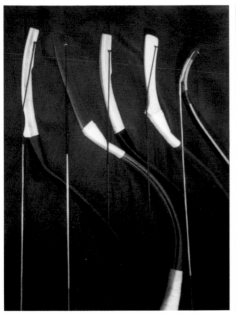

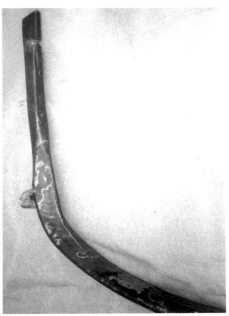

Five contrasting siyahs, a mini study
of five different angles and shapes of
siyahs. Left to right—Hun, Magyar,
Tall Magyar, Mongol, and Korean.

Chinese siyah, St. Charles Museum,
Seattle, Washington.

These five bows are modern productions made from modern materials,
and none was made using the three composite elements. The Korean made by
master Korean bowyer Bak Geuk-Hwan is very close in appearance to a genuine horn bow, while the others, all made by leading Hungarian bowyer
Kassai Lajos, show considerable departures.

Many ancient composite bows represented in bas-reliefs, paintings, or pot-
tery simply look like all-wood recurves or just deep-bending short straight bows
(without pronounced siyah formations), so it is difficult to date the invention of
the siyah. My best guess is that the siyahs appeared shortly after the time of
Christ, or at least by 200 to 400 A.D. with some certainty. The Scythian archers,
active around the beginning of the Christian era, had recurve-looking bows with
limbs ending in stubby, recurved tips that seem rigid, and therefore may have
been the embryonic emergence of the earliest limb-tip stiffenings to function as
a siyah (*The World of the Scythians*). However, much more certainly, silver plates
dating from 200 to 600 A.D. accurately depict demarcated siyahs; the siyah is

most clearly connected with the bows of the Huns (*The World of the Huns*). It is interesting to note that even though the simplest form of the lever dates back to around 2000 B.C. or earlier, the insight that it could enhance the performance of a bow lagged dramatically.

Uniting the Horse with the Bow

The union of horse and bow demands very special attention. Joseph Bronowski dramatically asserts that moderns have missed the revolutionary impact and upheaval of this union. When humans mounted the warhorse, they became twice as tall and menacing, three times as fast, and more mobile in orders of magnitude. Remember that ancient warfare from 1000 B.C. to 1600 A.D. and even later was largely face-to-face and intimate. Pageantry, visual display, and sound effects played a crucial part in stirring the fervor of your troops and planting mortal fear in the enemy.

The coming of the horse in modern form, Kassai Lajos of Kaposmero, Hungary.

If the blood curdling war cries of thousands of men advancing on foot was frightening, imagine what it was like when one witnessed for the very first time a thundering horde of mounted archers bearing down. Have you ever stood right at the rail at a steeplechase and felt the ground shake from the thundering hoofs? The horses and riders grow bigger, bigger, threatening to swallow you. The straining sounds of the thoroughbred's lungs fill the air along with the flying mud from their hooves.

Add to the looming height and sound of the attacking mounted archer other fearsome effects such as plumes on the horses' and soldiers' heads, rows of whirring feathers behind the riders' backs, high snapping banners and standards, pounding drums and screaming whistles, and the age-old war cry. And don't forget that word has preceded them about their deceptive lightning tactics, the power of their bows, and the pupil-smiting accuracy of their archers.

If you can now settle down a little, we'll describe a few select bows in some detail moving from the western perimeter of Asia, then eastward to Korea and Japan. We begin in Hungary.

The Magyar Bow

Currently, one of the most widely researched and re-created Asian bows within the western boundary of Asian archery is the Magyar or Hungarian bow. Its archeological record lies in the Carpathian Basin. The Basin was invaded by successive waves of horse-archers from the steppes of central Asia—the Scythians around the time of Christ, the Huns in 300 and 400 A.D., and then the Avars from 600 through 800 A.D. The Magyar tribes (later to be called Hungarian) entered the Carpathian Basin in late 800 A.D.; their origins have traditionally been centered in the forests of the Ural Mountains, but more current speculation locates them in the central Asian steppes. Both the Avars and the very early Magyars left an informative trail of archery remains, largely artifacts from graves.

A brief aside is in order here to further bring the horse cultures of the near East and central Asia to center stage. These were not just people who used the horse more than others; the horse was enmeshed into the very core of their being. A salient feature of fourteenth-century Muslim artistic renderings of the mounted archer is the complete unity of man and horse, and the equal size and importance of each. These people sat on horses from earliest childhood in order to tend their flocks, travel to better pasture and water, fight their enemies, and hunt for meat and skins. They also relied on the horse for milk and meat. In dire circumstances they even drank their blood. They must have been more like centaurs than the creatures of mythology. Horse racing and horseback riding exhibitions in the hippodrome (horse arena) was their equivalent of baseball, soccer, football, and auto racing all in one. The pair of horsetails and horse skulls posted by the door of their yurts reveals how their personal and tribal identity interlocked with the horse. In the cauldron of this horse culture, the horsebow was born and evolved.

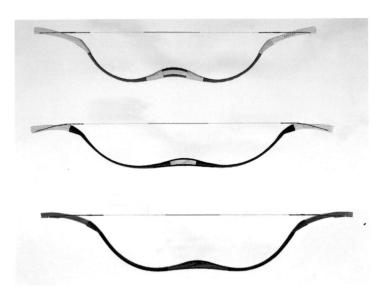

Three modern Magyar bows by Kassai Lajos of Hungary, from top, Magyar, Mongol, and Tall Magyar.

Now we go back specifically to the Magyar bow. The working part of the original Magyar bow is a composite of wood, horn, and sinew. The horse-archer was buried with his bow over his heart along with the head and shanks of his favorite horse and his saddle at his feet. The composite bow siyahs are bone plated and so are the bow handles. The sinew, horn, and wood have all decomposed over the centuries, but the bone plates are still intact when ancient Avar and Magyar graves are dug up and opened. It seems obvious that the properties of bone endure much longer than those of horn. The sampling of many undisturbed graves has developed a good picture of the length, contour, and positioning of these bone plates, and thus we have a good idea of the bow's overall configuration. This knowledge has been corroborated by pictures of these bows on clay, bronze, and silver table plates, bas-reliefs, paintings, and tapestries.

Dr. G. Fabian and Kassai Lajos have been some of the lead workers in researching and developing modern renditions of these ancient bows. Kassai Lajos also led the way in developing a standard and competitive mounted archery discipline. His bows are made in a modern shop in Kaposmero in the southwestern area of Hungary and shipped around the world. While his bowyers are at work, most of his time is spent at the Mounted Archery Valley, a couple of miles away. To be accomplished at a demanding sport like mounted archery requires rigorous daily training in heat and cold, rain and shine. Training new horses, teaching other aspiring mounted archers, and conducting competitions and demonstrations at home and abroad fill his schedule.

The Magyar re-creation is a symmetrical bow 51 inches (about 130cm) in length when strung, nock to nock. The siyahs are about 10 inches or 25 cm, long. The limbs are a high grade of Swedish fiberglass wrapped with various decorative leathers and often inscribed with ancient Hungarian symbols. Bands of cord wrapping are applied above and below the handle, and where the siyahs join the limbs.

The Kassai bow featured in the action photo below is actually his most recent rendition of the Hun bow, the historical forerunner of the Magyar. It is clearly asymmetrical—the bottom siyah and limb are noticeably shorter than on the top. It is beautiful, smooth, and accurate, and has a crisp cast. The siyahs are solid ash with overlays of a dark plum. The limbs have two laminations of action wood faced with clear fiberglass on the back and belly. The riser's inner portion is also dark plum, with a free-form bone inset. Traditional cord wrappings have been applied where the siyahs meet the limbs. In spite of this bow being 61½ inches (approx. 156cm), it is his favorite model for horseback archery.

Lajos in action with his favorite bow for mounted archery—the Hun.

Notice the very long Asian overdraw and the free-floating anchor in the photograph of the parting shot where Lajos is shooting at the target turned around backward. His release is the three-finger Mediterranean. Archeological evidence suggests that the ancient Avars and Magyars were about evenly split on using the Asian thumb-ring release versus the three-finger Mediterranean release. Again, artifacts leave a lot of room for conjecture and speculation. Perhaps the thumb-rings were just not included in burials, or perhaps they have decomposed.

The standardized European mounted archery course is 90 linear meters long with a three-faced target situated mid-way but nine meters to the left of the course. While at a fast canter or full gallop, an approach shot is directed toward the first face of the target, in the second third of the course, a right angle shot is fired at the second face of the target, and then the parting shot is released in the last third of the course. The course must be run in 16 seconds to qualify and at least one arrow must be attempted. An accomplished archer like Kassai Lajos shoots all three arrows in six seconds with a high hit rate. Accuracy and speed both contribute to the performance score.

The targets are 90cm (about three feet) in diameter, and the bull's eye is 30cm (about one foot). Remember that shots are taken at an action-packed full gallop, and must be taken at the highest rising point of each of the horse's strides. The archer may start a run with an arrow already nocked, carrying the two extra arrows in the bow hand and rapidly nocking them for the second and third shots. For the parting shot the archer is especially dependent on the mount's steadiness. One small, sudden jerk or sidestep at this point can unseat the best of riders and result in serious injury. Notice that the reins are dropped throughout the course, and the horse is self-guided.

The archer's bare shoulder is reminiscent of the same very formalized practice in Japanese Kyudo. The saddle style, with the high pommel (front), high cantle (back), and large round skirts, is also quite Asian.

Turkish and Related Bows

It would probably be unwise to say that any bow is at the apex of archery achievement, because each type of bow has a unique meaning to its owner. The special history, culture, religious meaning, and aesthetic of each world group establish their own archery traditions as the best from their own perspective. Nevertheless, Turkish products demand the honor and respect of all toxophilites.

While the modern re-creations of many other traditional bows may perform nearly as well as the seventeenth and eighteenth century Persian-Turkish bows, the Turkish bows have surpassed all others in terms of distance or flight shooting. A flight distance exceeding 400 yards is common for these hand-held bows. Apparently, the longest distance ever recorded was shot by the Ottoman Sultan, Selim III, in 1798. It exceeded 900 yards. For ultimate cast, *Saracen Archery* sets forth the proposition that the longer the siyah, the shorter the limb, and the more rigid and slender the handle, the better the cast.

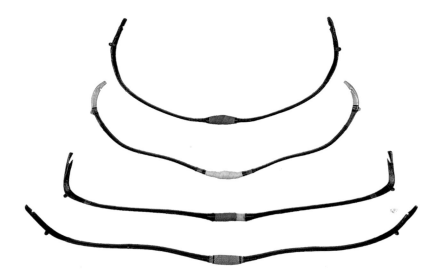

A comparative study of four bows, from top, Turkish, Indo-Persian, and two North Indian.

The Turkish records were reached with the extremely light barreled wood flight arrow, which looks something like a big toothpick about 26 inches long. These archers were assisted by a device called a siper; it was a trough strapped to the top of the bow hand that allowed the archer to draw the arrow well back

Crimean-Tatar (similar contour to Turkish) with the smoothly integrated siyahs, by Lukas Novotny of Ohio.

behind the belly of the bow. Thus, a very long powerful draw, coupled with an extremely short light arrow, could be achieved. These records all pertain to the hand-held bow shot in a standing position rather than with the archer lying on his back pushing the bow with both feet and pulling the string with both hands.

The Persian and Turkish bows also get a Blue Ribbon for aesthetics. They are meticulously covered in fine leathers and fabrics, or thin bark, and then lacquered as a waterproofer. They are set off with gold calligraphy or intricate, tiny, gold leaf designs, or a combination of both. Often the background colors are in subdued reds, maroons, or grays, all of which contrast artfully with the gold leaf painting. Often the calligraphy conveys one of the Forty Sayings from Islamic tradition about archery. Archery, held in the highest esteem in ancient Islam, received divine blessings. In terms of pure aesthetics, these weapons are superb works of art.

The Turkish bow shows a smooth transition between the siyahs and the limbs, while the Persian bow shows a little more demarcation. However, when

Indo-Persian with the radically angled siyahs by Lukas Novotny.

Tatar or Mongolian influence is added to these Near Eastern bows, the siyah then becomes visually more pronounced, longer, and more differentiated from the limbs.

The Karlsruher, Germany, collection of Turkish bows and other war materials is very large, well preserved, and impressive. The collection came from remains found on the battlefields from the 1600s and 1700s.

One of the leading researchers, bowyers, and reconstructors of the Persian, Turkish, and Turko-Tatar bows is Louis Novotny in the United States. He works with Kassai Lajos in the rebirth of mounted archery and is becoming a leading performer and promoter of the practice in the United States.

Indian Designs

Rama, the god-like figure of India, is often pictured standing and holding something similar to a longbow. The mastery of archery among the Indian aristocracy was similar to the courtly behavior of many cultures. The graceful, beautifully curved South Indian weapon was known as the "bow of the gods." If nirvana or heaven is a state of grace, perfection, balance, harmony, and wholeness, the aesthetics of the South Indian bow capture those characteristics.

The South Indian bow has been skillfully re-created and tastefully inter-preted by Jaap Koopedrayer from Ontario, Canada. The bow measures 62$\frac{1}{2}$ inches, or 159cm, from nock to nock when strung. Instead of using nock grooves, however, the string fits over the very end of the limb, which has been shaped down to a narrow tongue, and the string loop rests on a shoulder where the limb actually flares out wider, about $\frac{1}{8}$ inch on each side, instead of the usual tapering toward something like a point. The tongue-like structure at the very end of the limb is not unique; it was actually common among several North American tribes—the Powhatan and the Wampanoag in the northeast, and the Osage in the mid-west. This nock structure is also somewhat similar to that of the Japanese Yumi, as well as the Egyptian button nock, which is simi-lar but shorter and more rounded. The flaring shoulder is rare. From a side view one can see an extra piece of wood that has been added to the limb. It al-most looks like a brush nock, viewing it from the strung position.

The graceful curves of the South Indian bow.

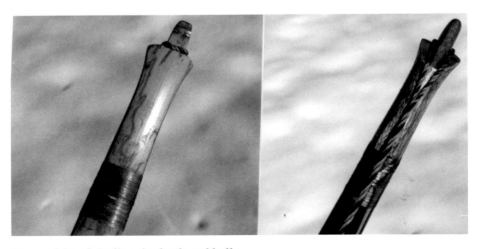

Unusual South Indian tip, back and belly.

Elegant gold-tipped Asian hornbow by Jaap Koppedrayer of Ontario, Canada.

Probably the most obviously graceful aspect of this bow is its five-curve configuration, a common configuration across many cultures. The proportions of the curves, however, are especially attractive and even more interesting because of the slight but noticeable asymmetry of the limbs; the upper limb is about two inches longer than the lower.

The handle treatments of these bows are a pleasure to the eye and to the hand. The grip is either sharkskin or leather wrapped diagonally with reed just above the grip, forming an arrow plate. The limbs are often set off with periodic ornamental sinew wrappings of fibers in contrasting colors. The back and belly of the bow are formed with a single layer of bamboo, and an exotic hardwood strip is visible on the side of the limbs. Very special versions of this bow will have rare naturally speckled or marked bamboo in the back and very expensive smoked bamboo on the belly. The widths of the limbs at the widest point are about 1³⁄16 inch. The shape of the limbs' cross section is a relatively flattened oval at the mid-limb position. The real surprise, however, lies inside this cocoon— four or five square laminations of bamboo running the full length of the bow, as in the seven-foot-long Japanese Yumi. The result is smoothness of shooting, durability, and a fine cast. That is why this is the "bow of the gods."

The North Indian bow is a very different piece. The North Indian bow was normally a true composite of horn, wood, and sinew with very pronounced siyahs set at an extreme reflex. It looks very much like the Mongol bows of the last couple of centuries in length and every way except for the extreme cant of the siyahs.

Chinese and Mongol Bows

Even though arrow points cannot always be distinguished from the smallest spear points cast by the atlatl, the remains of stone arrowheads in China suggest archery probably appeared there between 10,000 to 20,000 years ago.

Highly discriminating archery antiquarians would probably be uncomfortable with emphasizing the similarity of the Chinese and Mongol bows. An additional problem is that the Chinese bows pictured here are a century or two old, whereas the Mongol bows featured are typical of the current Mongol target bow. Moreover, as usual, generalizations are made even more difficult when keeping in mind that there is an array of variation within any tradition, each of which changes over time.

Nevertheless, similarities between the bows of the Chinese and the Mongols should be expected. For one, the lands border each other, and for the better part of the 1200s, China was forced to submit to the military rule of the Mongols. Exchange between the two cultures was unavoidable, and so it is likely that the impetus behind their two bows shared at least some commonality. Both types tend to be large or long when strung, ranging from about 55 inches, or 140cm, nock to nock to nearly six feet, or 183cm, in the very large Manchu versions. Both bows employ long, clearly demarcated siyahs, sometimes as long as a foot, or 30cm. Both use pronounced string bridges $1^1/2$ to two inches (5cm) long placed at the jointure of the siyah and limb. Both bows were horn, wood, and sinew composites. Both traditions used very long loops at the ends of the string made from sinew or gut, and the rest of the string was of multiple stranded silk.

One of the main differences in construction becomes apparent only when the bows are unstrung. The Chinese bow reflexes back to a "C" configuration when unstrung. The tips may still be two feet apart, however, and not nearly touching, as they often do in the Korean horn bow or the Turkish flight bow. The Mongol bow also reflexes when unstrung, but it's far less dramatic with the siyahs showing quite a bit of cant away from the archer, but with the limbs remaining nearly straight. The modern Mongol bow often has the limb wrapped with a clear nylon filament from the handle to the siyahs.

The making of the bow and the practice of archery have survived in Mongolia to this day. In fact, ground archery is one of the national sports featured at their yearly Nadom competitions held in early July; wrestling and horseracing are the other two national sports. Unfortunately, the same cannot be said for China. A few scattered bowyers struggled and scattered in China as late as the early 1940s, such as in Chengtu, but the cultural revolution under Mao-Tse-tung put an end to that. Fortunately, quite a large number of well-preserved Chinese bows remain from earlier periods in museums and in private ownership around the world, with some valuable artifacts remaining in China itself.

Former champion Mongol male archer, Inkbataar, showing the extended draw and clear profile of the typical contemporary Mongol bow made in Mongolia.

Mongol bamboo bow with dark, wood edges by Jaap Koppedrayer.

Korea

Korea, a relatively small country, is sandwiched in between massive China and powerful Japan. The size of the Korean bow is similarly diminutive, but like the Korean people, it has a great heart and life. Nock to nock, this little bow, when strung, is 45 inches or about 114cm. The size, configuration, and method of construction apparently have not changed much over several centuries.

Yet despite its size, this bow's cast is surprising to say the least, and measures up to the extremely long Korean target range of 154 meters. Its size and good cast are not its only marked characteristics, however. Its construction violates the Arab dictate of long siyahs and short limbs, but compensates with a relatively greater stiffness in the outer portion of the limb near the siyahs. This in effect makes the energy-producing portion of the limb shorter (from the handle to about one-third of the way out on the limb). So the deep curvature at full draw is not in the middle of the limb but closer to the handle. In addition, the outer limb's relative stiffness enhances the siyah's function, even though the actual siyah is only 4¼ inches, or 11cm, long.

At full draw the limb undergoes great stress, considering its shortness and narrowness, one inch, or 5cm. This would not be unreasonable in a long bow, but a bow this short calls for great care in construction, maintenance, and shooting.

Typical Korean target bow of wood, carbon, and fiberglass, with the back dressed in birchbark. Master Bak Geuk-Hwan makes an identical looking bow but in the old original manner from genuine water buffalo horn.

Thomas Duvernay, in old traditional Korean costume, approaches full overdraw using a thumb ring.

The original composite Korean bows required great skill, expertise, and patience to construct. While this is true of all horn bows, it's perhaps especially true here because of the vulnerability of that narrow, short limb.

The great care a bowyer must take can be seen in the meticulous process of gluing the horn on the belly of the bow. An exact and lengthy procedure of boiling and heating fish bladders must be followed in order to make the appropriate glue. Ten layers of this glue are applied every day for seven days, with stretches of time passing between applications. This is done in order to prepare a proper bonding bed on which to apply the horn. It is not surprising that many current Korean bows substitute a mix of fiberglass and carbon strips in the belly.

The Japanese Yumi

The very long seven- to eight-foot asymmetrical all-wood Yumi has the least similarity to any other bow in the world. The length actually varies anywhere from 83 inches, or 212cm, to 97 inches, or 245cm, depending on the

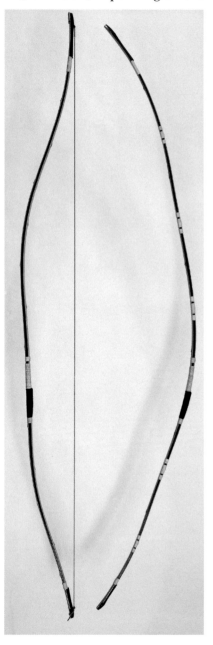

archer's height. Although Japan may have adopted the Chinese bow from the fourth to the ninth centuries, they rejected that pattern and turned to the long process of developing something all their own. By the fourteenth and fifteenth centuries, five-piece laminated asymmetrical limbs had come into common usage.

The unique Yumi lamination pattern still used today was established in the sixteenth century. The back and the belly of the bow are formed of two strips of bamboo in the almost universal manner of the lam running the full width of the cross section and full length of the bow. Sandwiched between the traditional back and belly, however, are five square bamboo strips (each about ¼ inch) running the full length of the bow. A hardwood strip is added to the two sides or edges of the cross section. This configuration is designed to prevent twisting, which is more likely in a very long and narrow bow, and it enhances smoothness and cast.

A very expensive Yumi is finished with over a dozen coats of urushi, a naturally derived Japanese lacquer purified from the sap of a tree in the sumac family. Some bows are wrapped at periodic spaces along the limbs with a reed.

When the gun replaced the bow and the practice of hunting waned on the

The great Yumi, unstrung and strung.

small, densely populated island, archery evolved into a highly ritualized martial art—Kyudo. The Shinto and Zen tenets of spirit, energy, concentration, discipline, and perfected behavior were all called up in Kyudo. Although some martial arts count self-defense among their objectives, all martial arts strive for self-development, emphasizing patience, restraint, humility, oneness, and control—perfecting timing, breathing, and movement.

One learns dramatically about one's own flaws, but one always envisions perfection, and improves toward that end. The expression, "Whether one thousand arrows or ten thousand, each one must be new" reveals what's at the core of the Kyudo frame of mind. Failure is not a disappointment, but an opportunity to move ahead and do better. Success, on the other hand, is never perfect, thus it is an opportunity for a new arrow, which will fly toward perfection. The archer learns from his failures, and supports his fellow archers in their improvement just as strongly. Above all, however, the archer's mind and spirit are maturing and growing ever so patiently into perfection.

So Kyudo, or "the way of the bow," becomes much more than a sport or hobby; it's a way of life. In the presence of the Yumi bow, the only descriptions available are simplicity, elegance, and depth, the same words that come to mind while watching the unhurried unfolding performance of Kyudo.

Don Symanski, Director of the Boulder Dojo in Colorado, ready to release the arrow.

Kyudo is learned and performed in a center called a Dojo. In Japan, it is common to see many high school students learning Kyudo as well as many older adult participants. Dojos are scattered more thinly throughout Europe and the United States, but they're usually present in any large metropolitan area.

The age-old practice of shooting the Yumi from horseback at a full-speed gallop, however, is much less common. This practice, called Yabusame, may reach back nearly 1,000 years, and is still alive in some locations in Japan, with a rare demonstration in other countries as well. The course is a straight track nearly 300 meters long. Several targets dotting the course on the left side are clay disks approximately five inches in diameter that crumble to the ground when hit. None of the targets are shot from a long distance, but all are hit at high speed when the archer rides by the target and releases his arrow. A wonderful two-minute segment of Yabusame is beautifully captured in the 1958 movie *The Barbarian and the Geisha*.

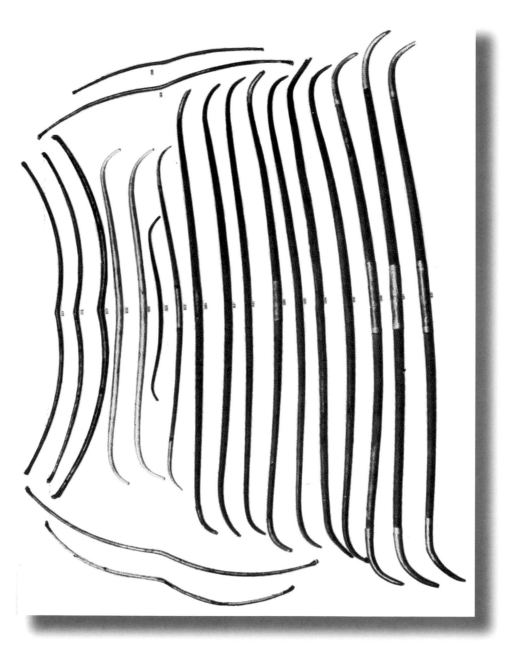

Fourteen self-bows and seven angular composite bows found in the tomb of Tut'ankhamun, from McLeod (1970). Copyright: Griffith Institute, Oxford, by permission.

5 · Africa

Up until very recently, the western world paid little attention to the history of Africa. This ignorance very likely derived from our modern prejudices, which can be as simple as, "Everybody knows there is nothing of cultural value in Africa, so why look there?"

However, it has become common knowledge that great civilizations rose and fell on the African Continent long before modern European nations were formed. While Africa is another rich storehouse of archery lore, unfortunately the records have not been uniformly well preserved. Even though the preserved record is spotty, and the current art of making and using the bow is sparse, there is ample evidence of a great legacy of archery. The exploitation during the colonial period and the political turmoil that has followed it to this day create anything but open access to the legacy. This chapter won't even scratch the surface, but I hope it is a testimony to the African archery treasury, and perhaps a challenge for more research and writing.

The Nubian archers

As far back as 3000 B.C., the land extending from southern Egypt to northern Sudan, and into western Ethiopia was known as Nubia. Although it was a harsh, hot, and dry climate, the larger kingdoms of Egypt and Rome soon noticed this land's riches—gold, ebony, ivory, incense, and more. A line of Nubian kings lived in the northern portion as early as, or perhaps predating, the Pharaohs. In this very early period, Nubia was known as "Ta Sety" or "The Land of the Bow" due to the prowess of its Nubian archers (1997, University of Chicago Website). The legendary accuracy of the Nubian archers, as well as other African archers, was so deadly that they were called the "pupil smiters."

Even if an enemy's armor is too thick to penetrate, after all, the eyes are always unprotected and vulnerable, which is perhaps the orgin of the Nubian reputation. In conflict with a Persian force in 3 A.D., the enemy fell to their deaths with arrows protruding from both eyes. Supposedly this was not just a matter of overcoming thick armor, but it was a point of pride and marksmanship (Heliodorus, account by Tukura, 1994).

It is reasonable to assume that the Nubian bow played a significant role in the country's domination of Egypt after her decline in 1100 B.C. Very dark-skinned Nubian Pharaohs ruled Egypt for nearly five hundred years, from 750 to 300 B.C. Following this period, the Nubians developed a world-class culture centered in the capital of Meroe, or Merowe, which lasted from 200 B.C. to 300 A.D. In fact a city by that name still lies about 150 miles north of Khartoum. All the usual archeological remains attest to a great civilization—royal city centers, palaces, temples, pyramids and other burial sites, and extensive urban remains.

Not much is known about Nubian archery equipment, except that their bows were very long—from six to seven feet. They were probably made from some variety of palm found on the banks of the Nile or acacia from the open bush country. The bows were supposedly hardened in fire.

Di Donato (1994) examined six Nubian bows in Turin, Italy's museum and discovered two differently shaped self-bows. One was a straight bow with some string follow, which was either man-made or the result of shooting. The other's shape is sometimes called a double curve bow, which actually has three curves; it's identical to the bow just described, except that there is an additional curve in the handle toward the archer, or set back. These six bows were between five to six feet in length, and may have drawn about 50 to 60 pounds. But the string attachment is particularly unique. In the process of bracing, the string was laid against the tip of the limb on the belly side, wrapped around the limb about 15 times, and then tucked under the last wrap. The bottom attachment was the same, although permanent.

Egyptian Self-Bows

The wood self-bows of the Egyptians were identical to the Nubian bows. How far back the Nubian design reaches we do not know. Tiny, finely designed flint tips suggest that some of the Egyptian bows may go back as far as 8000 B.C. The rather extreme bend of the tips toward the archer, with no obvious nocking groove, would seem to indicate it was very difficult to keep the string on the bow. The Nubian's self-binding string attachment described above (Di Donato, 1995) may very well be the answer to this puzzle. Fourteen of these self-bows were found in the tomb of Tut'ankhamun (McLeod, 1970).

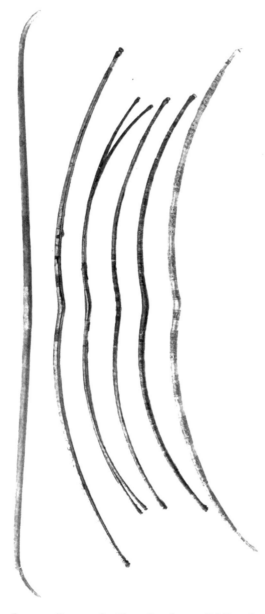

Composite angular Egyptian bows (McLeod, 1982). Copyright: Griffith Institute, Oxford, by permission.

Egyptian Angular Bows

The Egyptian bow that stokes the admiration of modern day archers is the composite, which appears in numerous bas-reliefs of fighting from chariots and boats, on foot, and even in hunting scenes. It is the invariable image of the archer at full draw. The string hand is pulled back well behind the ear, showing a very long arrow, and the bow's dynamic arc forms a full half-circle. Relatively short, it is widely accepted that this type of bow had to have a sinew reinforced back and a horn belly. The image alone is formidable, and the bow must have packed a fearful wallop. Hardy (1992) conjectures that they were probably imports from Asia Minor, and McLeod (1982) agrees, believing they were first acquired in Asia and then produced in Egypt. Some of the raw materials, such as elm wood, and cherry and birch bark, may also have been imported. This composite bow appears in Egypt during the age

Elaborate limb decorations on composite angular bows from the Tut'ankhamun tomb (McLeod, 1982). Copyright: Griffith Institute, Oxford, by permission.

of the Pharaohs in the Second Intermediate Period, which ran from 1570 to 1165 B.C. (McLeod, 1982).

Thirty-two of these composite bows, some in excellent condition, were found in King Tut's tomb along with a small number of self-bows. In these composites, horn and sinew were indeed combined with wood cores. The most frequent cross section seems to be nearly round or oval-shaped. The construction is what you'd expect—a wood lath in the core, with horn on the belly and a heavy body of sinew on the back. However, there are striking variations. For example, sometimes very thin horn strips are added on the back of the bow as well as the belly. Toying around with different arrangements of wood laminations in the core is also evident; one variation has small square wood lams similar to the core construction of the long Japanese Yumi.

The Egyptian Angular bow owes its unique appearance, when strung, to the triangle. The string is the hypotenuse, and from grip to tip the limbs are straight, which forms the sides of a triangle. The archer grips the valley of the triangle in the belly of the bow, and at full draw, the angle nearly disappears, and the limbs form a beautiful full half-circle.

The King Tut bows were discovered by anthropologist Howard Carter in 1923, under the aegis of the Griffith Institute of Oxford University, and were carefully preserved and documented during subsequent years. Museums around the world are now populated with these discoveries. There are major holdings in Luxor and in Cairo's Egyptian Museum, but they can also be found as far away as London and New York. But it wasn't until the Tut'ankhamun Tomb Series was produced in the 1970s and 1980s that the average English-speaking person had access to these reports and photographs.

The revered and elevated place of the bow during this period is expressed in the Tut'ankhamun collection as follows: "The good god, strong bow, possessed of might, vigorous in drawing it."

Bassa Bows

David Tukura tells one of the most complete and fascinating stories of the ongoing use of the bow in Africa. Tukura is a Nigerian, from the Bassa tribe, who did his graduate work in sociology in Canada. I'm most grateful for his chapter on African archery in Volume III of the *Bowyer's Bible*. David grew up learning the hunting and fighting stories of the Bassa, and he learned to love shooting the bow himself.

In a well-aged Bassa story of hunting a leopard, the bravery of the archers and the tightness of their social bonds are revealed. Failing to make a killing shot, an archer is attacked by a leopard. Rolling and slashing at each other on the ground, the archer is over powered. Finally, however, he is saved by the daring bravery of another hunter, his brother.

The Bassa identify with their Ethiopian brothers on the other side of the continent, where the following story occurs. When the Persian King Cambyses (c. 530-522 B.C.) sent spies to check out Ethiopia, the King of Ethiopia sent them home with a very heavy bow. The spies were to tell the King of Persia that when they had Persian archers equal to this bow, only then might they think of making war. "Till then," the Ethiopian king had said, "thank the gods for not turning the thoughts of the children of Ethiopia to foreign conquest."

The bows were made from small trees resembling black locust, 5 to $5\frac{1}{2}$ feet long, round or oval in cross section. The upper nock mechanism of the bow is most interesting. A hole is bored through the center of the belly of the limb, about $1\frac{1}{2}$ inches from the very tip. The string is slipped through the hole, back to belly, and knotted on the belly side. The nock groove is cut like the nock of an arrow at the very tip of the limb. When holding the bow in vertical shooting position, the archer looks through the open valley of the groove. When the bow is braced, the string is simply pulled up into the valley or saddle of the groove. Antelope rawhide is preferred for the string.

Similar to many of the old archery cultures, the bow was an integral part of the archer's identity. It was not something a person just did; it was a central part of who he was. The training and socialization into the bow started so young and so intensely, and the bow was so crucial in hunting and fighting for survival, that the unity of bow and archer is easily understood. And the heavier the bow you can pull, the higher your status.

Slave trade, as well as Islamic expansion, were apparently both markedly slowed by the persistent use of the bow by the Bassa and other tribes.

Elephant Bows

The Liangulu of Kenya are sometimes called "the elephant people." For decades they preferred the elephant for food. A concentration of them would camp at an elephant kill, feast on the meat, and dry large quantities of it. Later, in the 1940s, they were caught up in the ivory business and massacred hundreds of these revered animals, until 1948, when a large game preserve was established in southeastern Kenya to help stave off such poaching. A young game warden by the name of Frank Woodley recounts sighting flocks of buzzards and vultures, which usually led him to an elephant murdered primarily for its 70- to 100-pound tusks. Through uncanny sleuthing, he was able to get to the source of the killing and learn about the secretive Liangulu.

The Liangulu remained invisible by melding into many other tribes, but they developed a passion for elephant killing and the massive tools used for it. Woodley discovered they had been using bows as powerful as 130 pounds. Although he was a strong young outdoorsman, he could only pull these bows a few inches. The Liangulu had apparently developed the necessary arm and back muscles through years of conditioning. Dennis Holman (1967) conveys this relatively recent history in *Massacre of the Elephants*.

Kamba Bows

Strangely, the Kamba of Kenya also did some elephant hunting, but with three-foot bows pulling perhaps only about 50 pounds. I am not sure this mystery can be resolved with certainty. Both tribes relied on poison-tipped arrows, but the Kamba, or Akamba, were known for their pinpoint accuracy. If they could

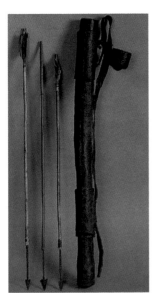

just penetrate the $1\frac{1}{2}$ inch skin, the poison would have its chance, albeit often slowly and dreadfully. And they may have depended on penetrating vulnerable spots—eyes, genitals, and the rectal area.

The bow shown here, however, is a beautiful specimen of tropical wood. It looks like aged rosewood, but is undoubtedly some native Kenyan wood. It is 47 inches long, perfectly round, and expertly tapered toward each limb tip, but it has a small horizontal fracture on the lower limb. The poison was applied to the detachable metal arrow points.

Akamba quiver of skillfully shaped and finely stitched leather. The detachable tips on the 20-inch arrows were often covered with poison.

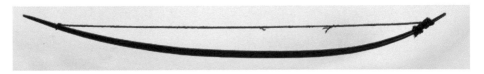

Akamba bow from Kenya, short but deceptive; capable of killing an elephant with poisoned arrows.

Inspired by the Great Lakes American Indian, this Winnebago or Potawattni-like bow is sinew-backed, by David Kissinger of Pennsylvania.

6 · The Future of Traditional Archery

The ancient past and the present of traditional archery taken together hold great promise for the future. Looking back over this very selective picture of bows of the world, how can we summarize what we have seen? I am impressed with three achievements in contemporary bows as well as the bows of antiquity.

Bows of the Past and Present

First, we are looking at *effective* weapons and implements of sport or self-development. They are instruments that have significant thrust or cast, with striking potential for accuracy. In exceptionally experienced hands, these bows can pluck a bird from the air, knock down a great beast in the field, or hit a small target at 50 or even 100 yards.

Secondly, these bows are *beautiful*. Even ancient examples—which are well sculpted, evenly finished, and have an artfully twisted or woven string, but are otherwise undecorated—are unequivocally works of art. The beauty of the object, even at rest, is part of the captivating nature of the sport. Add the act of shooting these works of art, and one is carried away with fascination.

Third, how could anyone fail to be impressed with the *variety* of design or the style of shooting? The bow ranges all over the boards—from very short to unbelievably long, narrow or wide, thin or thick, straight or bent limbs, parallel or compound curved profiles, a single piece of wood to a composite of many complementary elements.

These weapons are a profound tribute to bowyers and archers alike, ancient and modern. Great intelligence, sensitivity, and creativity are written indelibly across the limbs of all these great bows. This is not to diminish any of the other demanding physical sports or skills. It is just to say that archery by itself is a lucid testimony to the heights of the human mind and spirit around the world.

Bows of the Future

There is always the sentiment in traditional archery that everything that can be tried has been tried. And within this traditional practice there are boundaries to innovation. Nevertheless, there are new initiatives afoot, and there are probably other unforeseen ones out there in the future. The current combination of bamboo with other traditional woods in many different designs is worthy of mention. While these combinations have been common for centuries in some Asian traditions, the imaginative way western countries are using bamboo is relatively novel. It is being used in inner limbs and backs, and in belly treatments in longbows and recurves you'll find being made in the Americas

Master Sensai Shabata at full draw in the closing ceremony of a festival. The Sensai is in an unbroken twenty generation line of master bowyers and Kyudo practitioners. Sam West assisting.

and in Europe. Bamboo is definitely durable, and it seems to add smoothness to the performance without any loss in cast.

All-wood models are now appearing in designs which had previously been deemed impossible. Jaap Koppedrayer's bamboo/wood interpretation of the Mongol bow and Lukas Novotny's all-wood Chinese bow (fiberglass faced) are excellent examples. They are both rugged and perform well, with an added plus of great beauty and economy.

At the other edge of the traditional scene, new synthetic materials are and will be used. A number of bowyers are experimenting with thin carbon strips interspersed between wood lams. Bob Lee, founder of Wing Archery, gave us the first laminated takedown in 1952, and now gives us another newcomer—Durawood. He is impregnating hard rock maple with polymers in order to achieve more mass, strength, and durability. Some archers are even excited about the latest string innovations. Fast flight string can add several units of cast, (i.e. feet per send [fps]). As for arrows, to most traditionalists, metal and carbon arrows lie outside the realm.

New Levels of Information Exchange for Traditionalists

If this is the information age for most of the world, it is also the information age for archery. In the past—for several centuries, in fact—some archery books have always been available. The wonderfully rich *Journal of the Society of Archer-Antiquaries* has informed a limited number of international archers for over a half century. But the exponential growth of traditional archery in the last decade, coupled with instant communication via the Internet and e-mail makes this a truly exciting world forum for lovers of the flying arrow. An array of somewhat more popularized archery magazines disseminate news and ideas in what is really a quiet revolution. Their coverage is increasingly international in scope, and the widespread publication of *The Traditional Bowyer's Bible* is another part of this quiet revolution.

Many archer enthusiasts have direct or indirect access to the Internet, and cyber cafes have been making the Internet even more widely available. One may log on to atarn.org, the Asian Traditional Archery Research Network, and quickly tap into the vast world of Asian archery, thanks to the foresight and hard work of Stephen Selby from Hong Kong. Stickbow.com is more western oriented, but is an informal and quick way to see what others are doing and thinking for hunters and non-hunters alike. The rapidly emerging interest in mounted archery is also present on the Web with such sites as intlhorsearchery.org constructed by the Besheys in Port Dodge, Iowa.

Exchange of Equipment and Shooting

In the mid-1990s, one did not expect to see an authentic American Indian re-creation, or a Hungarian bow at any of the 3-D shoots. Likewise, it was almost totally unheard of for a hunting archer to shoot in a meet of the British Long-bow Society. Times have changed. Now, almost any kind of bow from almost any country may be seen. At almost any major traditional meeting or rendezvous, there will be archers, bowyers, and magazine editors from abroad. At my most recent major shoot, the person occupying the booth next to mine was born and raised in Germany, resides in Finland, and was selling Hungarian bows in the United States.

This mingling is even greater at the explicitly international events. Just watch the archers line up at the old-time Cherokee Cornstalk Shoot at the Fort Dodge International Archery Festival. Can you imagine seeing a seven-foot Yumi, next to a Hun, next to a typical American glass-backed recurve, next to an Austrian hornbow, and a number of Cherokee-made self-longbows? The mixture of origins of the archers matched all this mixture of bows. Can you imagine seeing two great masters of such radically different traditions as Kyudo (Yumis shot on foot) and Magyar mounted archery? The revered, fully costumed Sensai Shabata shoots an arrow only after the long, disciplined, and artful movement and ceremony of that martial art. In contrast, Kassai Lajos, in ninth century Magyar costume, has only six seconds to shoot three arrows from horseback while at a full gallop, revealing a radically different intense discipline.

Variety of Traditional Activities

Traditional shoots and rendezvous in the United States have tended to be-come somewhat stereotyped. The standard fare is a series of three-dimensional styrofoam animal target courses. Most often, the importance of keeping score has been minimized and the fun of it all maximized. These will always be great events as far as I am concerned. However, there are so many other kinds of events that could be used for variety, interest, and challenge. Events inspired by older European meets are occasionally appearing in the States—popinjay, clout, and the York Round, for instance. The Howard Hill shoot in Alabama in-corporates many moving targets, such as massive charging elephants and rhi-noceroses, and small undulating skunks and squirrels. Some competitive events with silver arrow prizes are being combined successfully with the non-competitive fun-oriented shooting that we never want to lose.

The emerging interest in mounted archery certainly adds a fundamen-tally new dimension and a burst of new excitement. Kassai Lajos gave the first demonstration ever in the United States at the Great Lakes Longbow Invitational in 1998. The response was spectacular, and it is slowly taking hold in this country. European mounted activity is still growing nicely, and we are beginning to see more international exposure of the well-established Japanese and Korean forms of this time-honored practice.

New Traditional Constituents

Youths and women have always been an important part of the traditional archery scene. The challenge of hunting, mounted archery, and shooting just for fun seems to be appealing to more women than ever. More organizations are holding special training sessions, hunting trips, and archery camps for youths, but overall the youth scene seems discouraging. Archery used to be a widespread and integral part of summer camps, and scouting. With adult concerns about liability, the video game fixation of many kids, and the time constraints of organized sports, youth archery is facing stiff competition. This should be a challenge to us all. It is not only the future of archery, but it is a great avenue to help develop the character of the next generation.

The use of the bow for violent warfare is mostly in the past, and sharp gender discrimination within traditional archery is rapidly fading. Archery is a viable and effective vehicle to nurture positive character. Kyudo and all the martial arts are about development of the self into a strong person of composure, restraint, balance, and beauty. The world religions uphold the direction of human perfectibility. The Christian expression of constant improvement is apropos here: "Be ye perfect even as your Father in heaven is perfect." The direction of our movement is critical. We will never reach perfection. We will always be flawed. But the goal of self-improvement is constant. The way of the bow is just one of many vehicles that can help you be a better person.

Yet, traditional archery is not a magic wand that will heal the ills of the past. Where there is the will, however, it is a rich field in which to grow new friendships across old forbidden barriers. The bows of the world warrant the celebration of character and achievement. They are portents of the good things to come.

References

GENERAL—Magazines and Journals

The Australian Archery Journal. Denali, Shallow Bay Road, Coomba Park, New South Wales 2428, Australia.

Le Chasseur a L'arc, 33, Rue de la Haie-Caq, 93308, Aubervilliers cedex, France. In French.

The Glade, The International Archery Magazine. 63 Hook Rise North, Tolworth, Surrey KT6 7JY, England.

Ijasz, Lap. 1461 Budapest, Pf.:33. Hungary. General archery magazine in Hungarian.

Journal of the Society of Archer-Antiquaries. Secretary E. A. Hart, 36 Myrtledene Road. Abbey Wood, London SE2 0EZ, England.

Primitive Archer, P.O. Box 79306, Houston, Texas, 77279-9306, USA.

Traditionell Bogenschiessen. Postfach 25 02 45, D- 67034 Ludwigshafen, Germany. In Deutsch.

Traditional Bowhunter. 208 North Latah, Boise, Idaho 837

Websites

commercial	information exchange
bbrothers.com	atarn.org
blueriverbows.com	bambooarrow.com

hwarangarchery.com

javamanarchery.com

krackow.com

kustom-king.com

salukibow.com

selfbow.com

3riversarchery.com

hornbow.com

horsebackarchery.com

intlhorsearchery.org

koreanarchery.com

sptradorch.org

stickbow.com

tradarcherycraft.org

Introduction

Bodio, S. (1998). *On the Edge of the Wild: Passions and Pleasures of a Naturalist*. New York: The Lyons Press.

Bradford, T. (Editor and Publisher). *The Glade: The International Archery Magazine*. England: Surrey.

Hamm, J. (1995). *Ishi and Elvis*. Azle, Texas: Bois d'Arc Press.

Kerasote, T. (1994). *Bloodties: Nature, Culture, and the Hunt*. New York: Kodansha Inc.

Thompson, M. (originally 1878, reprinted 1984). *The Witchery of Archery*. Walla Walla, Washington: Martin Archery, Inc. There is no best single book to whet the appetite for the beginning or older archer, but archers never cease to find the classic story of the Thompson brothers to be inspirational.

Chapter One: Prehistoric Bows

Alrune, F. (1992). A mesolithic elm bow approximately 9000 years old. *Journal of the Society of Archer-Antiquaries, Volulme 35*.

Alrune, F. (1996). Elm bows of prehistory. *Instinctive Archery Magazine, Spring*.

Alrune, F. (1996). The long elm bow of Vedbaek. *Instinctive Archer Magazine, Summer/Fall*.

Alrune, F. (1997). Ten bows from the sea bed: Artifacts from hunters more than 5000 years of age. *Instinctive Archer Magazine, Spring*.

Balee, W. (1995). *Footprints of the Forest.* New York: University of Columbia Press.

Bergman, C. A. *The development of the bow in western Europe*: *A technical and functional perspective.* I have this source in hand, but the bibliographical information is incomplete. It constitutes Chapter 7 in a larger work. The author is or at least was at Northern Kentucky University.

Callahan, E. (1996). The Holmegaard bow: Fact and fiction. *Instinctive Archer Magazine, Summer/Fall.*

Clark, J. G. D. (1963). Neolithic bows from Somerset, England, and the pre-history of archery in northwestern Europe. *Proceedings of the Prehistoric Society, Volume 29.*

Comstock, P. (1993). Ancient European bows. In Hamm, J. (Ed.), *Traditional Bowyer's Bible, Volume II.* Azle, Texas: Bois d'Arc Press.

Greenland, H. (1999). Meare Heath enigma. *Instinctive Archer Magazine, Winter.*

Greenland, H. (2000). English elm. *Primitive Archer, Volume 8, July.*

Hardy, R. (1992). The beginnings. In R. Hardy, *Longbow: A social and military history.* Azle, Texas: Bois d'Arc Press.

Heath, E. G. (1972). *The grey goose wing.* Greenwich, Connecticut: New York Graphic Society, Ltd.

Prior, S. (2000). Re-creating the Neolithic Meare Heath bow—reassessing the past through experimental archeology. *Journal of the Society of Archer-Antiquaries, Volume 34.*

Rausing, G. (1997). Historical survey. In G. Rausing, *The bow: Some notes on its origin and development.* Manchester, England: Simon Archery Foundation.

Rust, A. (1943). *Die Alt-Und Mittlesteinzeitichen Fun de Von Stellmoor.* Neumunster.

Chapter Two: The Americas

North America

Allely, S., and Hamm, J. (1999). *Northeast, Southeast, and Midwest.* Volume 1 of *Encyclopedia of Native American Bows, Arrows, and Quivers.* New York: The Lyons Press.

Bailey, J. (1995). The Penobscot bow. *Primitive Archer, Volume 3, Issue 4.*

Bailey, J. (1997). An American tradition for a thousand years. *Primitive Archer, Volume 5, Issue 1.*

Bailey, J. (1999). Bailey, J. (1999). The lost art of tillering the Penobscot bow. *Primitive Archery, Volume 7, Issue 1.*

Catlin, G. & Matthiessen, G. (Ed.). (1989) *Letters and Notes, North American Indians.* New York: Penguin Books U.S.A. Inc.

Ewers, J. C. (originally 1955, reprinted 1985). *The horse in the Blackfoot Indian culture: With comparative material from other western tribes.* Washington D.C.: Smithsonian Institution Press.

Fitzhugh, W. W., & Crowell, A. (1988). *Crossroads of continents: Cultures of Siberia and Alaska.* Washington, D.C.: Smithsonian Institution Press.

Gray, D. (1996). *The Krackow Company: The arts of international archery.* Cleveland: Schaefer Press.

Hamm, J. (1989). *Bows and arrows of the Native Americans.* New York: Lyons and Burford.

Hamm, J. (Ed.). (1992). *The traditional bowyer's bible, Volume I.* Azle, Texas: Bois d'Arc Press.

Hamm, J, (Ed.). (1993). *The traditional bowyer's bible, Volume II.* Axle, Texas: Bois d'Arc Press.

Hamm, J. (Ed.). (1994). *The traditional bowyer's bible, Volume III.* Azle, Texas: Bois d'Arc Press.

Herrin, A. (1989). *Cherokee bows and arrows: How to make and shoot primitive bows and arrows.* Tahlequah, Oklahoma: White Bear Publishing.

Kraft, J. C. (1986). *The Lenape: Archaeology, history, and ethnography.* Newark: New Jersey Historical Society.

Hamilton, T. M. (1982). *Native American bows, second edition.* Columbia, Missouri: Missouri Archaeological Society.

Laubin, R, and Laubin, G. (1980). *American Indian Archery.* Norman, Oklahoma: University of Oklahoma Press.

Mason O. T., and Fowke, G. (Original reports to Smithsonian, 1889-1893, reprinted 1995). *North American bows, arrows, and quivers, and chipped arrow heads.* Matituck, New York: Amereon House.

Pinney, D. (1998). Corn stalk shoot: How it's done. *Primitive Archer, Volume 6, Issue 2.*

Pope, S. (originally 1923, reprinted 1974). *Hunting with the bow and arrow.*Grayling, Michigan: Fred Bear Sports Club.

Smith, B. (1997). *How to make your own osage longbow.* Published by Brad Smith.

St. Charles, G. (1997). *Bows on the Little Delta.* Seattle: Glenn and Margaret St. Charles.

Thompson, M. (originally 1878, reprinted 1984). *The witchery of archery.* Walla Walla, Washington: Martin Archery, Inc.

Wallum Olum or Red Score: The migration legend of the Lenni Lenape or Delaware Indians. (1954). Indianapolis, IN: Indiana Historical Society.

Wissler, C., and Duvall, D. C. (1995). *Mythology of the Blackfoot Indians.* Lincoln: University of Nebraska Press.

Witthoft, J. (1990). *The American Indian as hunter.* Harrisburg: Pennsylvania Historical and Museum Commission.

South America

Baker, T. (1994). Bows of the world. In J. Hamm (Ed.), *Traditional bowyer's bible, Volume three.* Azle, Texas: Bois d'Arc Press.

Balee, W. (1993). *Footprints of the forest: Ka'apor ethnobotany—The historical ecology of plant utilization by an Amazonian People.* New York: Columbia University Press.

Biocca, Ettore. (originally 1965, revised 1996). *Yanoama, The story of Helen Valero, a girl kidnapped by Amazonian Indians.* New York: Kodansha Globe.

Chagnon, N. A. (1983). *Yanomamo: The fierce people, third edition.* New York: Rinehart & Winston.

Early, J. D., & Peters, J. F. (2000). *The Xilixana Yanomami of the Amazon: History, social structure, and population dynamics.* Florida: University Press of Florida.

Ferguson, R. B. (1995). A reputation for war. *Natural History, April.*

Good, K. (1995). The Yanomami keep on trekking. *Natural History, April.*

Hamilton, T. M. (1982). *Native American bows, Second edition.* Columbia, Missouri: Missouri Archaeological Society.

Heath, E. G., and Chiara, V. (originally 1977, reprinted 2000). *Brazilian Indian archery.* Manchester, England: Simon Archery Foundation.

Holmberg, A. R. (1950). *Nomads of the longbow, Publication number 10.* Washington, DC: Smithsonian Institute, Social Anthropology.

MacQuarrie, K. (n.d.). *Spirits of the rain forest.* Santa Monica, California: Family Home Entertainment.

Metraux, A. (1949). *Handbook of the South American Indians, Smithsonian Bulletin, Volume V.* Washington, D. C.: Smithsonian Institution.

Leaky, L. S. B. (1926). A new classification of the bow and arrow in Africa. *Journal of the Royal Anthropological Institute, Volume 56.*

Meyer, H. A. H. (1898). *Bows and arrows in central Brazil, Smithsonian Institute Annual Report, Publication number 117.* Washington, D.C.: Smithsonian Institute.

Chapter Three: Europe

Ascham, R. (originally 1545, reprinted 1995). *Toxophilus: The school of shooting.* Manchester: The Simon Archery Foundation.

Bradbury, J. (originally 1985, reprinted 2000). *The Medieval archer.* New York: Barnes and Noble.

Cenni, A. (1996). Wooden bows in medieval Italy. *Journal of the Society of Archer-Antiquaries, 39,* 50-51.

Cenni, A. (1997). Early Etruscan archery. *Journal of the Society of Archer-Antiquaries, 40,* 18-20.

Cenni, A. (Not dated). *L'arco e gli arcieri nell'Italia Medievale.* Greentime: Italy.

De Rham, C. C. (1990). *L'Abbaye de l'Arc de Lausanne, trois siecles de tir, 1961-.* Lausanne: IRL Imprimeries Reuenes.

Elmer, R. P. (originally 1926, reprinted 1993). *Archery.* Lyon, Mississippi: Derrydale Press, Inc.

Greenland, H. (1996). *The traditional archer's handbook: A practical guide.* Bristol, England: Sylvan Archery.

Hardy, R. (1992). *Longbow: A social and military history.* Azle, Texas: Bois d'Arc Press.

Heath, E. G. (1972). *The grey goose wing*. Greenwich, Connecticut: New York Graphic Society Ltd.

Hodgkin, A. E. (1951). *The archer's craft*. London: Faber and Faber Ltd.

Horn, J. (1932). The first international archery tournament. *Ye Sylvan Archer, 5*, 5-6.

Riesch, H. (1995). Archery in Renaissance Germany. *Journal of the Society of Archer-Antiquaries, 38*, 63-67.

Robin Sport Catalogue. Dorsten, Germany.

Robin Sport, Germany. www.robinsport.com

St. Charles, J. Pacific Yew. www.self.bow

Soar, H. D. (1994). The recreational longbow, Part I. *Primitive Archer, 2*(2), 20-25.

Soar, H. D. (1994). The recreational longbow, Part II. *Primitive Archer, 3*(1), 27-34.

Soar, H. D. (1995). The recreational longbow, Part III. *Primitive Archer, 4*(2), 39-47.

Chapter Four: Asia

"The Barbarian and the Geisha." (1958). [motion picture film on video]. Twentieth Century Fox.

Boudot-Lamotte, A. (1968). *Contribution a l'etude del'archerie Muslamane*. France: Institut Francais de Damas.

Bronowski, J. (1973). *The ascent of man*. Boston: Little, Brown and Company

Casson, L. (1965). *Ancient Egypt: Great ages of man*. New York: Time Incorporated.

Duvernay, T. (1996). Korean archery, The way of the bow. *Instinctive Archer Magazine, Spring*.

Elmy, D., & Wood, D. (2000). Present day traditional Korean archery. *Journal of the Society of Archer-Antiquaries, Volume 43*.

Farris, N. A., & Elmer, R. P., (Eds., Translators) (1945). *Arab archery: An Arabic manuscript of about 1500, "A book on the Excellence of the bow and arrow" and the description thereof*. Princeton, New Jersey: Princeton University Press.

Gray, D. B. (1999). The Magyar Bow and its People. *Instinctive Archer Magazine, Summer*.

Gray, D. B., & McCullough, J. (1999). Horse archers sighted in the United States. *Traditional Bowhunter, February/March*.

Grayson, C. (1993). Composite bows. In C. Grayson, *The traditional bowyer's Bible, Volume II*. Azle, Texas: Bois d' Arc Press.

Hardy, R. (originally 1976, reprinted 1992). *Longbow: A social and military history*. Azle, Texas: Bois d'Arc Press.

Heath, E. G. (1971). *The grey goose wing*. Berkshire, England: Osprey Publishing.

Hill, D. F. (1994). *An archer looks at the Bible*. Cambridge, England: The Pentland Press.

Hurst, G. C., III. (1998). *Armed martial arts of Japan: Swordsmanship and archery*. New Haven: Yale University Press.

Klopsteg, P. E. (originally 1934, enlarged 1987). *Turkish archery and the composite bow*. Manchester, England: Simon Archery Foundation.

Koppedrayer, K. I. (1998). Japanese arrowheads. *Instinctive Archer Magazine, Winter*.

Latham, J. D., & Paterson, W. F. (1970, based closely on an Arabic manuscript, undated, but originating somewhere within the late 1300s or 1400s.). *Saracen archery: An English version and exposition of a Mameluke work on archery, c. AD 1368*. London: the Holland Press.

Liptak, P. (1983). *Avars and Ancient Hungarians.* Budapest: Akademiai Kiado.

Maenchen-Helfen, O. J. (1973). *The world of the Huns: Studies in their history and culture*. Berkeley: University of California Press.

Onuma, H., DeProspero, D., & DeProspero, J. (1993). *Kyudo: The essence and practice of Japanese archery*. New York: Kodansha International.

Payne-Gallwey, R. (originally 1907, reprinted 1973). *Projectile throwing engines of the ancients, and Turkish and other oriental bows of medieval and later times*. Yorkshire, England: EP Publishing Limited.

Pant, G. N. (1978). *Indian archery*. Delhi, India: Dr. Agam Prasad.

Petarsch, E., Sanger, R., Zimmermann, E., & Majer, H. G., (Eds.) (1991). *Die Karlsruher Turkenbeute*. Munich: Hirmer Verlag.

Rausing, G. (1974). *The bow: Some notes on its origin and development*. Manchester, England: Simon Archery Foundation.

Rolle, R. (1989). *The world of the Scythians*. Berkeley: University of California Press.

Scidmore, E. R. (1904). *The Japanese Yano Ne*. London: The Japan Society.

Selby, S. (1998). The archery tradition of China. *Instinctive Archer Magazine, Spring*.

Selby, S. (2000). *Chinese archery*. Hong Kong: Hong Kong University Press.

Shelton, M. (1996). *Archery in Islam: A translation of forty Hadith on archery*. California: M. Shelton.

The Silk Road, Number 11: Where horses fly like the wind. A home video. (Date unknown). New York: Central Park Media Corporation.

Smith, G. Rex. (1979). *Medieval Muslim horsemanship: A Fourteenth-century Arabic cavalry manual*. London: The British Library.

Stein, H. J. (1988). *Kyudo: The art of Zen archery*. Longmead: Element Books.

T'an Tan-Chiung. (Paterson, W.F., Ed.). (1981 reprint). Investigative report on bow and arrow manufacture in Chengtu. *Soochow University Journal of Chinese Art History, Volume XI*, July. Found by Charles E. Grayson in 1951 based on reports in the 1940s, and translated by Charles E. Swineford.

Temesvary, F. (1995). *Diszes Nyergek, Loszerszamok*. Budapest: Dunakonyv Kiado.

Yadin, Y. (1963). *The art of warfare in biblical lands*.

Chapter Five: Africa

Adams, W. Y. (1977). *Nubia: Corridor to Africa*. Princeton, New Jersey: Princeton University Press.

Casson, L. (1965). *Ancient Egypt*. New York: Time Incorporated.

Cavalli-Sforza, L. L. (1995). *The great human diasporas: The history of diversity and evolution*. New York: Addison Wesley Publishing Company.

Di Donato, F. (1994). The Egyptian double-curved bow. *Journal of the Society of Archer-Antiquaries, 37*, 42-44.

Hardy, R. (1992). *Longbow: A social and military history*. Azle, Texas: Bois d'Arc Press.

Holman, D. (1967). *Massacre of the elephants*. New York: Holt, Rinehart, and Winston.

Leaky, L. S. B. (1926). A new classification of the bow in Africa. *Journal of the Royal Anthropological Institute, Volume 56.*

McLeod, W. (1970). *Composite bows from the tomb of Tut'ankhamun, Volume III.* In *Tut'ankhamun's tomb series.* Oxford, England: Griffith Institute of Oxford.

McLeod, W. (1982). *Self bow and other archery tackle from the tomb of Tut'ankhamun, Volume IV.* In *Tut'ankhamun's tomb series.* Oxford, England: Griffith Institute of Oxford.

(1992). Nubia Website maintained by the University of Chicago. Www.01.uchicago,edu/OI/PROJ/NUB/NUBX92/NUBX92

Owens, M, and Owens, D. (1984). *Cry of the Kalahari.* Boston: Houghton Mifflin Company.

Snow, F. M. (1983). *Before color prejudice: The ancient view of blacks.* Cambridge, Massachusetts: Harvard University Press.

Tukura, D. (1994). African Archery. In J. Hamm (Ed.), *The traditional bowyer's bible, Volume three.* Azle, Texas: Bois d'Arc Press.

Index